*"In Portugal, the **dogma of the Faith** will always be preserved etc."*

(Our Lady of Fatima, July 13, 1917)

Crucial Truths
to Save Your Soul

by Father Nicholas Gruner, S.T.L., S.T.D. (Cand.)

Immaculate Heart Publications
Buffalo, New York

ISBN: 1-896384-09-9

Please direct any correspondence expressing your concerns, questions or comments about *Crucial Truths to Save Your Soul* to the publisher at the following address:

Immaculate Heart Publications
Box 1028, Buffalo, NY, 14205

To order extra copies of this book,
Please write to one of the addresses below

In USA:

The Fatima Center
17000 State Route 30
Constable, NY, 12926

In Canada:

The Fatima Center
452 Kraft Road
Fort Erie, ON, L2A 4M7

Call toll-free: 1-800-263-8160
905-871-7607 | Fax: 905-994-7054
www.fatima.org | email: info@fatima.org

Printed in Canada

Dedication

To the Most Sacred Heart of Jesus,

Who shed all His Most Precious Blood for our salvation and Who continues today to nourish, sustain, encourage, urge and do all He can to save us despite our selfish, negligible, ungrateful response to His love.

To the unique Immaculate Heart of Mary,

so full of love for God and for each and every human heart that She became truly the Mother of God and also truly our spiritual Mother — generating each of us, who does not put obstacles in Her way, into the supernatural life of grace.

May this little book and all the limited efforts of The Fatima Center Apostolate contribute to the Triumph of Jesus and Mary all over the entire world — very soon.

Abbreviations

Dz.   Refers to the compendium of Creeds and Definitions assembled by the 19th Century German theologian Heinrich Denzinger.

D.S.   Refers to an enlarged edition of the Denzinger text made by Adolf Schönmetzer, S.J., known as the "Denzinger-Schönmetzer" text.

Table of Contents

Preface

by James Hanisch

I think mine has been a common experience among those who have been privileged to know Father Nicholas Gruner, and who have discovered Our Lady of Fatima's undiluted Message through his work at The Fatima Center. The refrain that I have heard repeated so often is essentially my own story: "If it weren't for that stranger who handed me a copy of *The Fatima Crusader*, I would never have found the truth of our situation in the Church today!"

If there has been anything unique about my own particular path to the true Message of Fatima — and to the true Faith and Traditions of the Catholic Church — it would merely be the intellectual density and laziness (or cowardice?) that kept me so long on the fringes of this battle.

In the mid-1990s, someone apparently submitted my name and address for a subscription to the *Crusader*. I was surprised to see it coming in the mail, and I wanted nothing to do with it. I had heard of Father Gruner — heard enough, as I supposed, to know that he was no good. He was a disobedient priest stirring up all kinds of trouble and division among Catholics. The Voice of authority in the Church had made it abundantly clear that "good" Catholics will have no part with Father Gruner.

That was enough for me. The wonderful thing about belonging to a hierarchical Church is that we laymen don't have to burden ourselves with the difficult questions touching our life as Catholics. That's what Church authorities are for, right? Or as Father Gruner says in the present volume, "Thanks, now I can go back to sleep!"

The *Crusaders* and other Fatima Center literature found little welcome in my home, but for some reason I kept them. It's hard for me to throw anything away, especially if it has nice pictures of Our Lord or the Blessed Virgin in it. I had stacks of things waiting for me to read, and it was a simple matter to start another stack — of things NOT to read.

Then one day I got a call from someone at The Fatima Center. A most courteous and well-spoken woman pointed out to me that I had been receiving the Center's mailings for some time, and asked if I might be willing to help support Our Lady's Apostolate.

This call was an uncomfortable challenge for me. Here I was, face-to-face (or voice-to-voice, as it were) with one of the erring and deluded people who had been intellectually and financially preyed upon by that bad priest, and I was painfully short of words. Sloppy thinking may suffice in the unexacting forum of our own minds (when we chose to allow the merest semblance of reasoning to pose as a justification for our actions), but such veneers are quickly seen for what they truly are when we face off with others in honest discussion.

I tried to explain to this woman that although I had not given the least advertence to The Fatima Center's publications or claims, I nevertheless knew enough to hold everything the Center did in the lowest possible regard. You can probably imagine the conversation. It was plain even to me that everything I said sounded quite foolish and irresponsible, and everything the woman said was on the mark.

In spite of the woman's patience and even kindness toward me as I struggled to explain what had seemed so clear until that moment, I ended the call feeling distinctly like a sham of a Catholic. Still, there was no question that the men in the Vatican wanted us laymen to have nothing to do with Father Gruner — why then did I feel as though I had not been doing my job as a Confirmed and committed member of the Church?

That question ate at me for a couple of days until I finally decided that enough was enough, and I pulled my copy of *Fatima Priest* out of the DO NOT READ stack.

"There's got to be a way to find out what this guy is about without having to read his whole book," I said to myself. Knowing that the Consecration of Russia was at the center of all the contentions surrounding Father Gruner, I went to the index and looked for entries under that heading.

Father Robert Fox, the safe and approved mouthpiece of the Church regarding Our Lady of Fatima's apparitions, was adamant that the requested consecration had been made in 1984. "Let's just see what inflammatory nonsense Father Gruner is spreading around," I said to myself, as I turned to one of the entries.

Page 72, citing the Blessed Virgin's own words in the great apparition of June 13, 1929:

> "The moment has come for God to ask the Holy Father to make, *in union with all the bishops of the world*, the consecration of *Russia* to My Immaculate Heart, promising to save it by this means."

Page 66, citing Abbé Pierre Caillon, head of the Blue Army in France:

> "In May 1936, in the course of an intimate communication, Lucy asked Our Lord why He would not convert Russia without these two so difficult conditions: that Russia should be the sole object of the consecration; and that this consecration should be made by all the bishops of the world, on the same day, each bishop doing so in his own cathedral in a solemn public ceremony. Our Savior replied: '*Because I wish all of My Church to recognize this consecration as a triumph of the Immaculate Heart of Mary*, in order, thereafter, to extend and place alongside devotion to My Divine Heart, devotion to this Immaculate Heart.'"

Page 84, citing an interview with Sister Lucy *a year after the 1984 consecration of the world*, published in the September 1985 issue of *Sol de Fatima*, the official journal of the Blue Army in Spain:

> "**Question:** At what moment of the Fatima mystery do we find ourselves?
>
> **Sister Lucy:** I think we are living in the time when Russia is spreading its errors throughout the world.
>
> **Question:** By that, are we to understand that Russia will take possession of the whole world?
> **Sister Lucy:** Yes.
>
> **Question:** John Paul II had invited all the bishops to join in the consecration of Russia, which he was going to make

at Fatima on 13 May 1982, and which he was to renew at the end of the Holy Year in Rome on 25 March 1984, before the original statue of Our Lady of Fatima. Has he not therefore done what was requested at Tuy?

Sister Lucy: There was *no participation of all the bishops*, and there was *no mention of Russia*.

Question: So the consecration was not done as requested by Our Lady?

Sister Lucy: *No. Many bishops attached no importance to this act.*"

Pages 214- 216:

"The Message of Fatima is not only a promise, but a warning. The promise has not been fulfilled because the warning has not been heeded: 'If people do what I ask, many souls will be saved and there will be peace. … If My requests are not granted, Russia will spread its errors throughout the world, raising up wars and persecutions against the Church; the good will by martyred, the Holy Father will have much to suffer, and various nations will be annihilated.' … Father Nicholas Gruner does not claim to be a Jeremiah. He has never claimed to be anything but a Catholic priest who can see what is manifest: that the promises of Our Lady have not come to pass, and that the fault cannot be Hers."

CRASH! All the walls of the Little House I had built in my imagination had fallen to the ground.

I was angry, yes, but as much at myself (for my own role in deceiving myself about the most important issue of our day) as I was at those churchmen who were actively propagating such blatant and deadly lies.

In a moment, having actually turned my own mind to the subject, it had at last become completely clear to me that all the bad press being levied against Father Gruner was the price which he was being made to pay for standing up for the truth — for Our Lady's honor, for the preservation of countless lives, and for the salvation of souls.

It was a scenario that we can all easily recognize because we are all routinely made to face choices of this kind on some level or another. Is there any working man, for instance, who hasn't at some time or other had to say to himself, as his stomach turned upside down: "If I do the right thing now, I will lose my job. What am I going to do?"

It takes a certain rare kind of individual to be faithful to Our Lord and to his own conscience when great sacrifices are required for that fidelity. I had never met Father Gruner, but I suddenly felt that I knew him quite well. The sheep can pretty easily distinguish a true shepherd from all the hirelings, especially when times are bad — there is just no other reason to explain why he would stay in the fight and allow the wolves to tear at him.

Outside of the Comfort Zone

Discoveries typically have a way of leading to other discoveries. My realization of where the right and wrong lay in regard to the continued need for the Consecration of Russia, was gradually followed by other broader realizations. Most importantly, I began to see that I had been the victim of a kind of shell game, in which the precious kernel of Revealed Truth, *the Dogma of Faith*, was being stolen from me, even while I thought I continued to possess it.

A shell game, when knowingly entered into, is an amusing challenge that tests both the dexterity of the one manipulating the line of shells, and the perception of the one watching the sleight-of-hand motions. One of several shells conceals a marble, and the observer is allowed to see under which shell it initially lies. Then the shells are rotated in a rapid series of sliding motions, left and right, across the table, during which the marble is cunningly passed from one shell to another. Finally, the observer is to guess under which shell the marble now rests.

In recent decades, the Catholic Faith itself has been treated like that marble in a shell game. In a happier day, it may have been that Catholics were able to rely on Church leaders without having to scrutinize issues for themselves. A good Catholic could say with assurance: "I'll follow Rome on this issue," or "I'm with the Pope," or "I believe implicitly all that the Church teaches in Her Sacred Councils." That same attitude today, however, could be disastrous. How can this be?

When the churchmen in Rome, beginning with the Pope, were dutifully teaching and defending the True Faith, and when the Councils in question had been *dogmatic* teaching organs, these assertions amounted to the same thing as saying, "I'll remain faithful to *the Catholic Rule of Faith.*"

But it has become all too apparent in our time that the words and examples coming from Rome — even from the Pope — may or may not be in line with the perennial and defined teachings of the Church. Nor do the teachings of the Second Vatican Council (a non-dogmatic, non-infallible *"pastoral"* Council) have any guarantee of orthodoxy.

In such a time, we dare not leave our thinking to others. The Catholic Faith, that "pearl of great price" without which we cannot be saved, will be taken from us unless we keep our eyes closely upon it. We must understand that truth does not change, and we must know how to distinguish the Church's true Magisterium from the happenstance utterings of present-day churchmen. In the diabolic shell game of these dark days, the losers will be those who despise the infallible definitions of Faith and follow instead the empty shell of a false obedience to the novelties preached by false shepherds.

That we live in such a time, when the Catholic Rule of Faith often no longer coincides with the utterances of the mitered heads in the Vatican and chancery offices throughout the world, was dramatically attested to by Pope John Paul II in his homily at Fatima during the May 13, 2000 anniversary pilgrimage:

> "The message of Fatima is a call to conversion, alerting humanity to have nothing to do with the 'dragon' whose 'tail *swept down a third of the stars of heaven*, and cast them to the earth.'"

Not exactly a model of plain speaking, but nevertheless clear enough — the Third Secret of Fatima (which Our Lady expressly ordered to be published for the Church at large by 1960, sufficiently in advance of the Second Vatican Council and the scandal-ridden liturgical revolution that came in its wake) is an explicit warning to the faithful *against an injudicious confidence in the pastors of the Church*, many of whom in our time will have fallen into the service of the devil! A diabolical snare of a false obedience is being exploited by the enemies of our souls to change the beliefs of Catholics, in order that the dogma of the Faith will no longer be preserved in this world!

Sister Lucy, the surviving visionary of the Fatima apparitions, endured a ban of silence for the last forty-five years of her life, from about 1960 until her death in 2005. In her personal letters during that period, however, this warning against blindly following untrustworthy churchmen was her recurring theme:

"Unfortunately, in religious matters the people for the most part are ignorant and allow themselves to be led wherever they are taken. Hence, the great responsibility of the one who has the duty of leading them....

"Our poor Lord ... has saved us with so much love and He is so ... little loved! So badly served! It is painful to see such a great disorientation and in so many *persons who occupy places of responsibility* [in the Church]! ... They are *blind leaders of the blind*, ... as Our Lord tells us in His Gospel, and souls go on allowing themselves to be deceived. Gladly I sacrifice myself and offer my life to God for peace in His Church, for priests and for all consecrated souls, especially for those who are so deceived and misled!"

But if the Catholic Rule of Faith is not just whatever the reigning Pope or Church prelates *say* it is, then what exactly is it? What are the sources of dogma to which we can all refer and which bind the entire Church for all time, from the throne of Peter to the back pew? How can the faithful be taught to make these distinctions for themselves between Revealed Truth and novelties, between true and false obedience, and thus be able to keep their eyes on the Pearl instead of on the shells?

An Evening with Father Gruner

After many years of following and supporting The Fatima Center's work, I was at last privileged to meet Father Gruner and even to spend several hours with him one evening in April of 2013. We discussed these very questions at length, circling round and round what we believed to be the crux of the problem: The faithful need someone to spell these things out for them from the ground up, from both a theological and historical perspective. If only there were a brief and simple booklet available demonstrating that the true Catholic Rule of Faith is not arbitrarily subject to the whims and fads of a "living magisterium," and that no churchman of any rank has the "authority" to change Revealed Truth or to undermine the good of the Church.

But, of course, even if such a booklet existed, we realized, the real work would still be ahead, and it could only be done by the faithful themselves. They would have to nerve up to the task of educating themselves about what it truly means to be a faithful Catholic, and then act upon that understanding. The temptation would always be to take the effortless route, staying in the mindless-obedience comfort zone, and insisting that as long as they are "with the Pope" they can't be wrong. If only more people realized that the Message of Fatima was a warning from Heaven not to make that deadly mistake! The booklet would have to demonstrate this as well.

Thus it was during that dinner conversation (which went late into the evening) that the idea for this present book was conceived. (Hence the rationale for Father Gruner's gracious invitation for me to write this Preface.)

I wish that I could give the reader some idea of that very memorable conversation. Father spoke with such feeling as I will never forget:

> "It has happened twice in the history of the Church that the Magisterium has been dimmed — first during the Arian heresy, and now again in our time. Our time is as desperate — or worse — than the period of the Arian heresy, when the devil came very close to destroying the Church. I believe that today the devil has come closer to destroying the Church than he did then.

So many people say, 'Oh, that was what the Church taught before Vatican II,' as if it were a small matter to set aside the teachings that Our Lord commissioned the Apostles to preach to all nations until the end of time! The truth cannot contradict itself, nor can the Church contradict Herself, nor can the Magisterium contradict itself throughout the centuries. If we lose the Faith that the Church has always taught, we lose our souls!

People need to have the principles in front of them. Then they will be able to deal with all the questions that challenge their faith. They have to understand that the Church's true Ordinary and Universal Magisterium can never be in opposition to the solemn definitions of the Extraordinary Magisterium. This has to be explained in a way that everyone can understand.

So many Catholics seem to have the idea, 'If the Pope said it, you have to obey. Period.' No, if the Pope commands something *within his jurisdiction*, we have to obey. *There is a limit to the Pope's authority.*

If the Pope tells you to go and live in Timbuktu, you are perfectly free to say, with all respect, 'No, thank you.' Now, of course, the Jesuits take a vow to go wherever the Pope sends them, so if you happen to be a Jesuit, that would be a different matter. But the Pope does not have the power to command ordinary Catholics in this way. And if the Pope orders you to profess that there are four Persons in the Blessed Trinity, you don't have to obey him. You *must disobey* him. You must resist him. Period.

People have to understand this. Pope Paschal II's bishops understood. When he told them to do something that would have compromised the Church, they said: 'No, we're not going to do that. End of discussion.' And soon afterward Paschal himself admitted that they had been right.

The authority given to the Pope and to the bishops is not a power to confine the Gospel, but to preach the Gospel.

They don't have any authority to hinder the Gospel. That's the reality, and that's what the people have to understand. It's not enough for a churchman just to say something, and suddenly it's law. No, he can command only in matters within his jurisdiction and only within reason for the common good of the Church. It is not enough for true Catholics to say, 'Oh, well, we have to accept whatever the Pope and bishops say.' No, that is no service at all to Our Lord or to the Church.

Saint John Gualberto, an 11th Century Italian abbot, knew that the Bishop of Florence was a scoundrel, who had paid gold to be appointed to his powerful position. St John denounced him as such. He called on God as his witness and he worked a public miracle, sending one of his monks through a trial by fire. (That monk is a canonized saint, too — Saint Peter Igneus.) The people then drove the simoniacal bishop out of office with their pitchforks! That was a true service to the Church.

If people were only to read the lives of the saints, they would be amazed. The saints weren't canonized for serving Our Lord with the kind of spineless piety that most people imagine them to have had.

Saint Columbanus is another example. He was a 6th Century Irish monk who spent much of his life as a missionary in Gaul (i.e. France). His influence was feared by the French bishops, who were enjoying the luxuries of their office and doing nothing to advance the Faith among the pagans. They weren't interested in preaching the Gospel, but they didn't want anyone else doing so on their turf. So in the year 602 the bishops summoned Columbanus to appear before them and answer to them about what he was doing. There they all were, assembling with so much solemnity to judge him, and he simply went on with his work. He sent them a respectful but frank letter, encouraging them to do their job while he continued to do his. Columbanus is the canonized saint, and those bishops… who knows where they are? Let's hope they're in Heaven, but no one even knows their names today, while the whole Church will go on honoring Saint Columbanus for his example of zeal and holiness until the end of time.

People have got to realize that God expects them to use their brains. I'll never forget the experience I had as a seminarian in the diocese of Montreal. Someone in the chancery office — not the Cardinal Archbishop himself, but some lower functionary — issued a letter stating that as of January 15, 1967, it was forbidden to promote the message of Garabandal in that diocese. Or rather, it *didn't* say that. But when you read the letter, that was the *impression* that you got. That was the obvious import of the letter, at least on the first reading. I happened to read the letter through a second time, and as I did, I realized that nowhere in the letter was any such order actually given. It was abundantly clear that the Chancellor or whoever wrote the letter (I can't remember now who signed it) wanted the reader to believe that this order had been given, but I looked up and down the letter, and there was simply no explicit order anywhere in it.

I spoke to the Vice-Chancellor (whom I knew, and who happened to be living in the seminary where I was studying), and I asked him: 'The first time I read this letter, I understood it to forbid certain activities, but the second time I read it, I saw that no order of any kind is actually given. Did I miss something?'

I learned much more about theology and Canon Law from his answer than I've learned in many hours spent in some seminary classes. It was a very sad lesson to have to learn, but every Catholic needs to hear this. He said: 'You understood the letter correctly. We purposely wrote it that way.'

They deliberately created the impression of giving a formal order, binding under obedience, but they never actually gave the order!

This is a lesson in spades for everybody, and people need

to learn this lesson. Why is this such an important lesson? *Because that's how the Church has been run in many places, including at times the Vatican, for the past fifty years!* In all manner of things, they beguile the Catholics who look to Church leaders with simplicity and trust. These leaders insist that you must obey, but they will not take responsibility for giving the command. That's what they did with all of the ambiguities of the Second Vatican Council and with the New Rite of Mass. They insist that these novelties are authoritative Catholic teaching, and that it is forbidden to go to the Traditional Mass, but they don't dare to actually decree what they know is not true, and what is impossible in Catholic dogma and Church law.

No Pope since the time of the Second Vatican Council has ever come out and said, 'I declare, define, and pronounce that everything proposed in the Council documents is Catholic dogma.' They don't dare attempt such a thing. And yet they do say: 'You must *obey*. You must sincerely accept in your heart with religious submission whatever the Council has taught.'

That's false! Saint Thomas explains why nothing false can come under the virtue of faith. We cannot be commanded to believe something that is false. They are asking for a sinful false obedience, and Catholics need to be able to recognize this distinction.

Pope Paul VI never said that the Old Mass was forbidden, but he allowed the people around him to claim that he had forbidden it, and to create that impression among Catholics throughout the world. The Popes have stood by silently for the past fifty years while their underlings have gone around claiming: 'You must do this and that. The Pope says you must obey.' They create the *impression* of due process and then demand obedience to commands for which no one takes responsibility and which in actuality have no basis in Church teaching or law.

God bless Pope Benedict for having the courage to finally correct this false notion that the Traditional Mass had been forbidden. In his *Motu Proprio* of 2007, the Pope reversed the lies coming out of Rome for the previous forty years, very plainly acknowledging what the Society of St. Pius X and others like Michael Davies had maintained all along — that Paul VI never abrogated the traditional Missal, and that priests and the faithful have never needed 'permission' to continue in the traditional rite. It has always been permitted by the law of the Church! So we can thank Pope Benedict for telling Catholics the truth about that much.

The Traditional Movement is not just about being traditional or appeasing individual preferences for old ways. It's about the truth, which cannot contradict itself. It's about the Catholic Faith itself — a dogma of the Faith. It has been solemnly defined, in Session 7 of the Council of Trent [Canon 13 on the Sacraments in General, Dz. 856, D.S. 1613], that we are bound in conscience to the traditional rites of the Church. No pastor of any rank whatsoever (including a Pope) can replace the received and approved rites with a new rite.

Popes Paul VI and John Paul II both attempted to publish new missals for the Church, in a rite which Paul VI himself admitted was a "new rite" [*Cf.* Nov. 19, 1969 General Audience address and Apr. 3, 1969 Apostolic Constitution *Missale Romanum*, §13], and which Cardinal Ratzinger confirmed was no development of the Roman Rite, but a fabrication, a construction [*Cf.* Preface to *The Reform of the Roman Liturgy* by Msgr. Klaus Gamber]. But neither Paul VI nor John Paul II had the authority to replace the received and approved rite with the New Mass. *No one* has that authority. *That's a defined Catholic dogma!* We are all bound to the traditional rites that we have received from prior generations. This is what it means to hold onto the Faith. This needs to be said so clearly. To this day, that has not been said by anyone clearly enough for people to get the point. That's why we need Our Lady's words in the Secret. Not just the vision, but Our Lady's words as well. That's the text we need.

Pope Pius XII knew Our Lady of Fatima's warning. We all need to hear it in Her own words — that, as he said, the Message of Fatima is a divine warning against the suicide of altering the Liturgy. Our Lady said that to alter the Liturgy would be *suicide* for the Church. To change the Mass would be to try to change the Faith into something else, and beyond being an attack on the dogma of the Faith, it would be catastrophic for the Church.

But we're talking about more than just Vatican II and the New Mass. They have done this in so many things. They give the impression to priests that they must give Holy Communion in the hand, but if you read the decree it doesn't say that at all. It says the opposite! It says that the law of the Church *forbids* you to give Communion in the hand unless an entire set of impossible conditions is satisfied. But the impression given to every last member of the faithful, from the bishops to the First Communicants, is that Communion in the hand is the norm of the Church.

They tell the world that the Pope consecrated Russia to the Immaculate Heart of Mary in 1984, and they constantly invoke the Pope's authority for that claim, but John Paul II never claimed that he had done so. In fact, he said the opposite on the front page of *L'Osservatore Romano*.

This is the tactic that the subversives are using to destroy the Church, while we sit back and say, 'Well, they're in charge,' when we should be saying: 'With all due respect, Your Eminence, or Your Excellency, I cannot obey you in this. You don't have that authority.' They have no such power to undermine the faith and salvation of souls! Really, God is in charge, and yes, He has given limited authority to the leaders of His Church, but not a license to destroy the Church if they so please.

People have to understand what's going on in the Church today. This is such a crucial point for people to understand about obedience. This is key, and it is criminal that our leaders are deceiving people in this way. They are criminals to do that. Maybe some of them don't have any sense of how wicked a thing it is to do what they are doing, but the faithful need to be shown that we are in no way bound to cooperate in the irreligious schemes of the Modernists, regardless of any number of hollow orders from high-ranking churchmen.

To his credit, the Vice-Chancellor of Montreal explained to me exactly what he was up to. Most of them won't be that honest. I don't think he understood just how malicious the technique is. I'll describe it with its proper term: it is *schismatic*. They are tearing the Church apart. They are creating disunity. That's what schism is. The unsuspecting faithful have formed judgments based on the falsehoods coming out of Rome or out of the chancery offices, and now we see all sorts of division in the Church. The law of the Church says that the Traditional Mass can never be forbidden, but these churchmen have created the impression that it is forbidden, and so we have people fighting with each other, even within families: 'You're disobedient! You're not Catholic! You're excommunicated!' It is all due to the schismatic 'orders' given from Rome. The simple Catholics, who haven't given the matter any thought or study, assume that they cannot be schismatic as long as they follow Rome. That's not true. Schism normally arises from inferiors, but Catholic theology is clear about this, that even a Pope can be the author of a schism.

These diabolical double-tongued orders cannot be allowed to continue to deceive Catholics. We need to find a way to explain this to them in such plain terms, with such a clear presentation, that they can't miss the point. There's got to be some way to get this truth out to the people!"

It struck me repeatedly as we spoke that Father's words were the expressions of a true father who was grieving and worrying over the plight of his wayward and endangered children, whose salvation was being undermined at its very foundation, as John Paul II affirmed. Father Gruner's anguish over the state of the

Church was evident, and I recognized in his anguish the same familiar pain that every parent knows so well.

In that famous homily given at Fatima on May 13, 1982, in which Pope John Paul II linked the Message of Fatima to an *undermining of the foundations* of our salvation, he also said that it was impossible that Our Lady of Fatima could silently endure such a scandal to afflict Her children, without rousing Herself to intervene:

> "Can the Mother, Who with all the force of the love that She fosters in the Holy Spirit and Who desires everyone's salvation, can She remain silent when She sees the very foundations of Her children's salvation undermined? No, She cannot remain silent."

Nor, we might add, can anyone who is in a real sense the father of these same children keep silent in such perilous times, when the dogma of the Faith is being lost in a growing apostasy. I warmly thank Father Gruner for bringing this idea for a book into a reality. May Our Lady deign to bless it and to prosper it according to the desires of the loving father (Her own Fatima Priest) whose labor of love it has been.

Introduction

by Andrew Cesanek

If one word could describe the depth and breadth of the crisis in the Catholic Church today, it would be *confusion*. But not just any confusion, for here we are dealing with confusion about Divine Revelation, the very Truth that makes us free and leads us to eternal salvation. For this sort of confusion Sister Lucy of Fatima had a very powerful description, no doubt inspired by her knowledge of the Message of Fatima and the Third Secret in particular: "diabolical disorientation."

It is hardly "fear-mongering" or "doom-saying" to speak of diabolical disorientation in the Church today. Someone as respected as Monsignor Klaus Gamber, whose critical study of the New Mass was highly praised by Cardinal Ratzinger before he became Pope Benedict XVI, was just as dramatic as Sister Lucy in his assessment of the current condition of the Church:

> "Great is the confusion! Who can still see clearly in this darkness? Where in our Church are the leaders who can show us the right path? Where are the bishops courageous enough to cut out the cancerous growth of modernist theology that has implanted itself and is festering within the celebration of even the most sacred mysteries, before the cancer spreads and causes even greater damage? What we need today is a new Athanasius, a new Basil, bishops like those who in the fourth century fought courageously against Arianism when almost the whole of Christendom had succumbed to heresy."

In his essay *On Consulting the Faithful in Matters of Doctrine*, Cardinal Newman gave a description of the Arian crisis in the Church during the 4th Century, when it seemed almost the whole Church had come to deny the divinity of Christ. His description certainly reminds us of the situation we are now witnessing in the Church:

> "The body of bishops failed in their confession of the Faith…. They spoke variously, one against another; there

was nothing, after Nicea, of firm, unvarying, consistent testimony, for nearly sixty years. There were untrustworthy Councils, unfaithful bishops; there was weakness, fear of consequences, misguidance, delusion, hallucination, *endless, hopeless, extending into nearly every corner of the Catholic Church*. The comparatively few who remained faithful were discredited and driven into exile; the rest were either *deceivers or deceived*."[1]

Cardinal Newman's essay shows how the laity, clinging to *the defined dogmas of the Faith*, along with a few good bishops such as St. Athanasius, were able to keep their faith alive during the Arian crisis. They did so not by deciding for themselves what the truth is, but rather by following what the Church has always taught and what the Catholic Church had defined once and for all. This is precisely the lesson which Catholics today must learn — to follow the defined dogmas of the Faith, regardless of the errors of so many of their peers and even of their leaders in the Church.

Catholics today must cling to the Catholic creeds of all time — e.g., the Nicene Creed, the Athanasian Creed, the Creed of the Council of Trent. They must cling to the Catholic Faith as taught by the Ordinary and Universal Magisterium — the faith of all time as found, for example, in the Catechism of the Council of Trent.

The Arian situation was similar to other periods of crisis in the Church, such as during the height of the Protestant revolt, when (particularly among the English clergy) Catholics found that even their pastors and bishops had lost the Faith. So it is today, when throughout the Catholic world members of the faithful have been left on their own to provide a sound Catholic formation for their children, while even schools called Catholic often pose a threat to the Faith which they are supposed to be teaching.

This book has been written from the perspective of the Message of Fatima, which warns us about what will take place in the Church after the year 1960, when the Third Secret of Fatima was supposed to have been revealed to the world but instead was suppressed. We know the Virgin of Fatima's warning about the coming crisis

---

1   John Henry Newman, *On Consulting the Faithful in Matters of Doctrine* (Kansas City: Sheed and Ward, 1961), p. 77.

in the Church begins with the words Sister Lucia recorded in her Fourth Memoir: "In Portugal, the dogma of the faith will always be preserved etc." Sister Lucia's "etc" holds the place for the rest of what Our Lady revealed, which we have yet to see. But what we can see is that it relates to *Catholic dogma* first of all, a failure to preserve belief in "the dogma of the Faith" in places other than Portugal — many places.

In fact, speaking precisely of the Message of Fatima, in 1931 the future Pope Pius XII, then Cardinal Pacelli, declared that Heaven itself has given the Church a warning about such a catastrophe in the Church:

"I am worried by the Blessed Virgin's messages to Lucia of Fatima. This persistence of Mary about the dangers which menace the Church is a divine warning against the suicide of *altering the Faith, in Her liturgy, Her theology and Her soul....*"[2]

The future Pope went on to make this frightening prediction in the light of Fatima:

"A day will come when the civilized world will deny its God, *when the Church will doubt as Peter doubted.* She will be tempted to believe that man has become God."[3]

The day whose coming Pius XII feared is now clearly upon us. In this time of doubt, confusion, indeed "diabolical disorientation" in the Church, it falls to each of us to hold fast to what we have received in the Church's infallible teaching on faith and morals. We must do this no matter what anyone says to the contrary, and no matter how high his office in the Church. That is why this book has been written.

---

2   Msgr. Georges Roche, *Pie XII, Devant L'Histoire* (Paris: Editions Robert Laffont, 1972), p. 52.

3   Ibid., p. 53.

Dear Reader,

Your eternal salvation or damnation could depend on reading this book! I beg you to read it closely, cover to cover.

The Third Secret begins with Our Lady of Fatima's words, "In Portugal, the dogma of the Faith will always be preserved" — thus Our Lady clearly implies (as She may well have gone on to say explicitly in the remaining part of the Secret) that the dogma of the Faith **would not** be preserved in other parts of the world.

As Our Lady of Fatima warned, such a loss of faith would bring an incalculable loss of souls as well. It cannot be otherwise, because preserving the dogma of the Faith is necessary for salvation. Our Lord tells us: "He who does not believe shall be condemned." (Mark 16:16) If we lose the Faith, we lose our soul!

The attack on Catholic dogma and the resulting widespread loss of faith predicted by Our Lady of Fatima is now well underway throughout the world. The dogma of the Faith has been so ruthlessly attacked that it is in danger of being lost altogether throughout entire nations and continents.

Truly, in all its glorious history, the Church has never suffered such losses in its numbers or in the integrity of its witness to the world as has occurred during the past half-century (beginning in the 1960s, when the Third Secret and indeed much of Our Lady of Fatima's entire Message were shamelessly despised throughout the Church at large).

Even from high places within the Church, the true Faith is attacked and contradicted, and many of the faithful are blindly following their blind guides (i.e., bad priests, bishops, and Cardinals) toward the pit of heresy and apostasy. If these misled faithful continue to the end on their present paths, they could follow their blind guides even to hell.

There is much confusion today about what the Church actually teaches. Many Catholics have learned, for example, that with a little shopping around, they can find a priest who will tell them that there is no sin for married couples to use contraceptives. Yet decades before this same unnatural sin became the pandemic that it is today even among practicing Catholics, the Catholic Church had made its teaching absolutely clear and explicit: Every instance of thus frustrating the natural end and procreative power of the marital act is grievously sinful, as Pope Pius XI declared in his 1930 encyclical *Casti connubii*.

In our perverse age, it is only those who love the Truth who will be saved. The rest will have no difficulty finding all manner of salves for their conscience, making it easy to exclude God from their lives. Soon they will not even be aware that they have begun to believe the lies which they preferred to the truth! Having chosen for themselves the seduction of iniquity, they will be handed over by God to a deceiving influence. (2 Thess. 2:10) God will not be mocked by our craftiness in throwing off His Commandments. "With the sincere, God is sincere; with the astute, God is astute." (Ps. 17:26)

It was a maxim of Saint Padre Pio that if we refuse to believe in modern-day miracles, we will end up not believing in the miracles recorded in the Bible. Why is this so? How can it follow that a skepticism in regard to real miracles in our own day will lead to a shipwreck of the faith, refusing to believe in the Revelation of Sacred Scripture, meriting eternal punishment in hell?

The First Vatican Council affirmed that miracles — not just those of biblical times, but also the miracles which God has continued to work throughout the ages as a testimony to the truth of the Gospel — are in themselves a sufficient motive of belief in the Church's teachings. (Canon 3, §4; Dz. 1813) If we choose to deny the dictates of human reason, disrupting the natural basis of belief within our own minds, we will undermine the very process by which we come to make the mind's supernatural assent of faith.

Those who prefer to cling to the humanistic euphoria of the 1960s rather than to accept the somber Message of Our Lady of Fatima, choose to ignore the testimony of 70,000 witnesses of the Miracle of the Sun. They ignore also the prophecies of Our Lady which have already been fulfilled, proving the truth of Her Message.

It is easy to recognize the follies of previous generations. But the folly of our generation surpasses them all. To this very day, the vast majority of Catholics have failed or refused to take Our Lady of Fatima's Message seriously enough, for whatever reason. Ultimately, I believe, people simply do not want to bear the inconveniences attached to living up to this Message — the great purity required of a truly Christian life, the special devotions to the Immaculate Heart of Mary that God wills us to embrace, and the generous spirit of penance and reparation which Our Lady asks of us. Simple things, really, which God makes easy to bear. But Our Lady's Message has been generally despised, and the result, as Saint Padre Pio indicated, has been a loss of faith, and on a broad scale.

Our world is in grave danger today because of the sin of despising Our Lady of Fatima, and our souls are in grave danger as well. Saint Paul warns us not to "extinguish the Spirit" by despising the true prophets sent to the Church by the Holy Ghost:

"Extinguish not the Spirit. Despise not prophecies. But prove all things, and hold fast to that which is good." (1 Thess. 5:19-21)

The apparitions and Message of Our Lady of Fatima have been thoroughly tested by the Church, and found to be good. To despise Fatima is, therefore (according to the expressed rule of Sacred Scripture), to extinguish the Spirit.

Sister Lucy stressed this identical warning to us in her 1957 interview with Father Fuentes, that to reject the Message of Fatima is to sin against the Holy Ghost. She warned that by ignoring the Virgin of Fatima's prophetic Message, we would preclude the hope of any pardon from Heaven:

"[I]n the plans of Divine Providence, God always before He is about to chastise the world, exhausts all other remedies. Now, when He sees that the world pays no attention whatsoever, then, as we say in our imperfect manner of speaking, He offers us with 'certain fear' the last means of salvation, His Most Holy Mother. It is with 'certain fear' because if you despise and repulse this ultimate means we will not have any more forgiveness from Heaven because we will have committed a sin which the Gospel calls the sin against the Holy Spirit. This sin consists of openly rejecting with full knowledge and consent, the salvation which He offers. Let us remember that Jesus Christ is a very good Son and that He does not permit that we offend and despise His Most Holy Mother. We have recorded through many centuries of Church history the obvious testimony which demonstrates by the terrible chastisements which have befallen those who have attacked the honor of His Most Holy Mother how Our Lord Jesus Christ has always defended the Honor of His Mother."[4]

Our Lord has punished the world (and Catholics in particular) for not accepting the Message of Fatima, and He is perfectly just to do so. The fault of this widespread outrage against the Mother of God does not lie only with the subversive clergy who abuse their authority and influence and who discourage obedience to Our Lady's requests. Why has the vast majority of the faithful placidly gone along with these crimes — the silencing of Our Lady's Message, the silencing of Sister Lucy, and the silencing of any priest who clearly, openly strives to proclaim the truth of Fatima?

If you refuse to seek, embrace, defend, and promulgate the truth of the Message of Fatima, then you deserve the coming great chastisements described by Our Lady, including wars and natural disasters, and even the satanic New World Order which is about to be cruelly imposed on all mankind.

Our faith is in danger today from more than just the base influences of the world, the flesh, and the devil — in our time, we are in danger even from influences within the Church. Our faith is undermined by the bad example of our fellow Catholics, and even by the most insidious snares laid by bad Cardinals, bishops, priests, and religious. In this time of diabolic disorientation, when even the elect could be deceived (if that were possible), we must be on our guard against the lies of a false, betraying clergy, lest we be taken in and lost for our sloth, our spiritual laziness, our lack of effort to

---

4   Frère Michel de la Sainte Trinité, "Sister Lucy's Conversation with Father Fuentes (December 26, 1957)", *The Whole Truth About Fatima,* Volume III: *The Third Secret* (Buffalo, New York: Immaculate Heart Publications, 2001), pp. 507-508.

learn, understand, and live the truth of the Catholic Faith.

We must be faithful to prayer, and particularly to our daily Rosaries, which Our Lady of Fatima in our time has made unprecedentedly powerful. Knowing also that our faith is under attack, we must likewise take care to preserve and strengthen our faith. Failing to preserve our faith would mean the end of our relationship with God, and therefore also the loss of our eternal reward with God in Heaven!

Truth does not change. If we wish to save our souls, we must persevere in the true Faith — the same dogmatic truths of Faith which the Church has always taught, and which are found especially in the Church's infallible definitions. We must not allow ourselves to be deceived by the lying novelties of a New Theology invented by a faux magisterium disconnecting itself from the perennial Faith of the Church.

A diabolical disorientation is operating all around us, deceiving many highly-placed priests and bishops and Cardinals of the Catholic Church around the world as well as powerful officials of similar or higher rank even in the Vatican. These deceived, ignorant officials and deceiving Judases are making victims too of countless lay men and women. We must love and defend the true Faith; we must love and defend and live the Message of Fatima. Otherwise we will very quickly face not only the end of our world, but an uncertain eternity as well.

I have written this book out of love for you, dear reader. My words are intended for all those who wish to remain truly faithful to Jesus Christ, to His Holy Mother, and to the teachings of the Catholic Church. Please say a prayer before you read this book, asking Our Lady of Fatima to enlighten your mind beyond my abilities to communicate Her Message to you. Ask Our Lady to touch your soul, opening it to all the movements of grace that She wants to inspire in you by the words of this little book.

Neither you nor I asked to be born into this perverse generation, so sadly characterized by confusion of minds and by silence on the part of too many of our leaders, if not by their ambiguous and equivocal leadership. Please approach the "radical" message of this book with an open mind. As Sister Lucy said to Father Fuentes, it is necessary now for each one of us to begin to reform himself spiritually:

> "Father, we should not wait for an appeal to the world to come from Rome on the part of the Holy Father, to do penance. Nor should we wait for the call to penance to come from our bishops in our diocese, nor from the religious congregations. No! Our Lord has already very often used these means and the world has not paid attention. That is why now, it is necessary for each one of us to begin to reform himself spiritually. Each person must not only save his own soul but also all the souls that God has placed on our path."[5]

Let us all humbly admit to ourselves that we may have been deceived by the diabolical influences of our day, to the extent that some of our most fundamental assumptions need correction.

It was God's loving and infallible Providence that placed us in this dark time, here and now, and if we are faithful to God, He will surely be faithful to us. "Seek, and you shall find," He tells us. (Luke 11:9) If we truly seek the truth, we will not lack the grace we need to find it. I pray that you and I and all who read this book will finish our individual journeys through this life free of the errors and snares and blasphemies of our age, and rejoice together in Heaven forever.

Father Nicholas Gruner

Father Nicholas Gruner

---

5 *Op. cit.,* p. 506.

Chapter 1

You Must Love the Truth – You Must Embrace Fatima

St. Paul tells us that a love of the truth is foundational, as a necessary condition to save our souls and to advance in the spiritual life. The seduction of error and sin, he says, gets all its power over souls from this one cause, that they do not have a love of the truth:

> "And in all seduction of iniquity to them that perish; because they receive not the love of the truth, that they might be saved."[6]

This is something for each of us to consider. We all have our blind spots, especially in the way that we see ourselves. We all have emotional pre-dispositions that we are liable to act on, rather than on real thinking, unless we are careful to distinguish our feelings from true judgments.

Real thinking is harder than simply acting spontaneously on our emotional responses. But that is our job as the "rational animals" in this world. We have to think things through, and we have to have an attitude of "Truth first."

I was in St. Peter's Square on October 13, 2013, expecting to see Pope Francis consecrate the world to the Immaculate Heart of Mary, as he had announced during the previous August. From the moment the ceremony began, however, I began to suspect that the plans for the consecration had been changed.

Those of us close enough to see the Holy Father's chastened and dour expression — completely uncharacteristic of him — realized that something had happened. It was as though someone in the Vatican, whom the Pope didn't dare to oppose, had "schooled" him about political correctness in regard to Marian devotions.

Had he just been told that a consecration to the Immaculate Heart of Mary was not allowed?

The ceremony was very brief, and the Immaculate Heart of Mary was not so much as mentioned. In fact, the Holy Father did not consecrate anything.[7]

But that disappointing ceremony was not the only misfortune of the day. As I prepared to leave St. Peter's Square, a certain woman (whom I had never met before) recognized me and made her way through the crowd to where I was standing, and she proceeded to give me an earful about her opinion of my work at The Fatima Center.

She introduced herself as a representative of the World Apostolate of Fatima (which most people still refer to as the Blue Army), and she scolded me at length for all of my apostolate's "misdirected" efforts to bring about the Consecration of Russia as specifically requested by Jesus and Mary. In her estimation, my publishing the truth that the Consecration has not been done, serves only to "hurt the Pope."

To her thinking, apparently — and there are many who might agree with her — I was being disloyal to the Church by insisting on Our Lady of Fatima's *requests*, whereas only the *devotions* to Our Lady of Fatima are relevant today. Such people often accuse me: Why must I keep talking about the release of the rest of the Third Secret? Who am I to insist on the explicit Consecration of Russia

7   His special prayer that day was as follows:

"Blessed Virgin Mary of Fatima, with renewed gratitude for Your Maternal presence, we unite our voice with that of all the generations who call You blessed. We celebrate in You the great works of God, Who never tires to incline with mercy toward humanity, afflicted by evil and wounded by sin, to heal it and save it.

"Accept with the compassion of a Mother, the act of entrustment which today we make with confidence, before this Your image to us so dear.

"We are certain that each one of us is precious to Your eyes and that nothing which dwells in our hearts is unknown to You. Let us reach Your sweet gaze and receive the consoling caress of Your smile.

"Guard our life in Your arms: bless and strengthen every good desire; revive and foster faith; sustain and illumine hope; create and enliven charity; guide all of us in the path of holiness.

"Teach us Your same preferential love for the small and the poor, for the excluded and the suffering, for sinners and the lost: gather all under Your protection and give all of us to Your beloved Son, our Lord Jesus." Cf. "Pope Francis' Prayer Entrusting All of Us to Our Lady of Fatima", *The Fatima Crusader*, Issue 107, Fall 2013, p. 12 (http://www.fatimacrusader.com/cr107/cr107.pdf#pg12).

to the Immaculate Heart of Mary by the Pope and all the Catholic bishops of the world?

These people have a very simplistic (and profoundly un-Catholic!) rationale for their position: We have been told that 1) the Vision of the "Bishop dressed in White" is the whole Third Secret, and 2) the Consecration was done in 1984; now we should concentrate on prayer, penance, and our own more-complete conversion.

The woman from the "World Apostolate" was basically demanding that I join the ranks, and say like all the false friends of Fatima[8] and those millions of souls deceived by those blind leaders that the Consecration has been done and that the Third Secret has been published in its entirety. (If she didn't insist that I *speak* such falsehoods, she clearly wanted me to do so by my silence.) Then I, too, could have the satisfaction of being truly "devoted" to Our Lady, since I would be "loving" the Pope and fostering the "unity" of the Church.

Well, Saint Louis de Montfort wrote a beautiful book about **true** devotion to Our Lady, and nowhere does he speak of serving Her *by serving a falsehood*!

Would I be showing any real devotion to Our Lady *by going against Her and Jesus' express will* that Her Fatima Message be made known and Her requests be fulfilled? Would I be loving the Pope by standing idly by when I know that he is about to lose his neck unless he repents and heeds Our Lady's commands? Is there any value in the kind of unity that Pilate and Herod achieved when they set aside their former enmities and united to crucify Jesus Christ?!

If a person's supposed devotion to Our Lady is not based on the truth, then it is not a true devotion. If a person's love of the Pope is not based on the truth, then his "love" is an illusion. If a person's efforts fostering the "unity" of the Church are not based on the truth, then he is building a house of cards. Our Lord did not build His house upon a bed of lies, and He needs no lies to support His holy Church.

---

8   There are various persons and groups of people who claim to be promoting Our Lady of Fatima's Message but who do so in a deceptive manner, wherein they falsify the true message. See Christopher A. Ferrara, *False Friends of Fatima* (Pound Ridge: Good Counsel Publications, 2012).

There was so much that I wanted to say, but in the end, it wasn't much of a discussion. This woman essentially blocked her ears and said "I do not want to argue with you" whenever I tried to say something. In her mind, I was upsetting the equilibrium of the Church and disrupting the unity of the minds of the faithful; therefore, I was in the wrong. Period. No further discussion is allowed. Except for her to repeat her insolent verbiage.

I wished I could say to her: "Please, Ma'am, what if Cardinal Bertone's Party Line about the Third Secret and the Consecration of Russia *is not true*? Should we ignore Our Lady's warnings and requests, for the sake of an appearance of unity among ourselves? At the risk of our lives and souls?!"

But the few words that I managed to get out simply echoed back to me, having bounced off of a brick wall.

Even if I had been able to say more, I knew I wouldn't be able to change this woman's mind, because she was concerned above all with the *appearance* of "love for the Pope". The *truth* of our situation was simply not her concern. So many people like her put the appearance of "love for the Pope", of "unity" and of "obedience" above the truth.

In fact, failing to put a love of the truth first, and above all other considerations, is the essence of many of the problems of our day. This is the fundamental disorder that has been at the root of the Church's disobedience to the commands of the Queen of Heaven for more than eighty years.

"Everyone That Is of the Truth, Heareth My Voice"

Ever since 1988, certain Vatican officials have been pushing the idea that we need to separate the *devotional* aspects of the Message of Fatima from the *prophetic* parts of the Message. It's been an organized campaign,[9] in which the idea of this separation has

---

9   Fatima historian Frère François writes: "[In 1988] an order came from the Vatican addressed to the authorities of Fatima, to Sister Lucy, to diverse ecclesiastics, including Father Messias Coelho, and a French priest very much devoted to Our Lady [evidently Father Pierre Caillon], ordering everyone to cease pestering the Holy Father with the Consecration of Russia." (Frère François de Marie des Anges, *Fatima: Tragedy and Triumph*, Immaculate Heart Publications, 1994, pp. 189-190.) In the same place, Frère François cites this statement from his personal correspondence

been forced onto the faithful. The message has been, in effect: "The consecration requested by Our Lady was done in 1984. Stop pestering the Holy Father about the Consecration of Russia!" The idea (which they clearly want to establish) is that it would somehow be *disloyal* or *divisive* for us to ask the Pope to perform the Consecration or to release the full text of the Third Secret.

So it's not uncommon now to find people (like this woman from the "World Apostolate" of Fatima) who think that the *prophetic* Fatima Message, which calls for the Consecration of Russia and for the release of the full Third Secret, is in some way *opposed* to the *devotion* to Our Lady's Immaculate Heart, as requested by Our Lady of Fatima.

Obviously, there is no real opposition between loyalty to the Church and obedience to Our Lady. But how is it that such an opposition could appear to exist?

The answer to that question is very simple. It is because people do not understand the essential duty that each of us has, to love the truth.

In fact, the more we truly love Our Lady, the more we will love the truth. Jesus said of Himself that He is the Way, and the Truth, and the Life.[10] Our Lord also said, as He stood before Pilate, that everyone that is of the truth, hears His voice.[11]

Why is it that being "of the truth" is the essential condition of being able to respond to God's voice? Our Lord explains this in a beautiful parable given in the Sermon on the Mount:

> "The light of thy body is thy eye. If thy eye be single, thy whole body shall be lightsome. But if thy eye be evil thy whole body shall be darksome. If then the light that is in thee, be darkness: the darkness itself how great shall it be!"[12]

Saint Thomas Aquinas can help us to understand this parable.

with Father Pierre Caillon, the President of the Blue Army in France: "An order came from Rome, obliging everyone to say and think: 'The Consecration is done. The Pope having done all that he can, Heaven has deigned to agree to this gesture.'" (Letter of March 1990)

10   John 14:6.

11   John 18:37.

12   Matthew 6:22-23.

He says[13] that the light of reason performs the same role for our souls as our eyes perform for our bodies. That is, our hands and feet themselves cannot see. Of themselves, they have no way of knowing their surroundings. The "light" for all the various parts of our body is simply having a healthy set of eyes in the same body.

Our eyes, receiving the light of day, enable all the members of the body to be properly directed in their tasks. Our hands work confidently and accurately, and our feet are sure, when enlightened by "single" or good eyes. On the other hand, if a person's eyes are unhealthy, then all the members of his body are reduced to act as though they were in darkness, even if that body were in broad daylight.

The situation is the same for our souls, St. Thomas says. If our minds are oriented to the light of truth, then all our judgments of mind and movements of will are able to be enlightened. But if our reason is misdirected — inverted, giving the highest place to earthly things — then all of our mental faculties will also be misdirected and in darkness.

To Love the Truth Is the Most Important Thing

Fatima is about the truth. Our Lady came to Fatima to put an end to the devil's empire in this world, which is based on the *lie*. Lies are the very foundation of his kingdom on this earth, because it is by lying to men and women that he is able (if they believe his lies) to enslave them to his will.

Jesus tells us that the truth has no place in the devil. The devil's lies follow naturally from this — namely, that he is not in the truth, and the truth is not in him:

> "He was a murderer from the beginning: and he stood not in the truth, because truth is not in him. When he speaketh a lie, he speaketh of his own: for he is a liar, and the father thereof."[14]

Those who do not put the love of truth above all earthly goods, put themselves in the same great darkness in which the devil reigns.

13   *Cf.* St. Thomas Aquinas, *Commentary on the Gospel of St. Matthew*, trans. by Rev. Paul Kimball, Dolorosa Press, 2012, p. 273.

14   John 8:44.

If we do not "stand in the truth," then neither are we "of God." The words of Our Lord Himself bore no fruit when they fell on the ears of such men:

> "Why do you not know My speech? Because *you cannot hear My word.* You are of your father the devil…. If I say the truth to you, why do you not believe Me? *He that is of God, heareth the words of God.* Therefore you hear them not, *because you are not of God.*"[15]

Again, Fatima is about the truth. Whenever Our Lord and Our Lady come to us, it is to bear witness to the truth,[16] which will make us free.[17] The devil comes to enslave us with his lies, sometimes even disguised as an angel of light.[18] He has been known to impersonate Our Lady in false apparitions in order to draw people's attention away from Our Lady's true message in Her true apparitions. (The devil appeared in at least 16 different places not very far from the town of Lourdes in 1858, under the guise of the Blessed Virgin, when Our Lady was appearing at the grotto of Lourdes to St. Bernadette.)

Always remember that lies enslave us, and that the truth is from God for the salvation of our souls. The lies being told today about the Message of Fatima come ultimately from the devil, who wants to prevent us from hearing the truth of Our Lady's Message, which — if we respond properly to it — could save countless lives and souls.

When Our Lady said, "*If what I say to you is done, many souls will be saved and there will be peace,*"[19] She was telling us the truth. When She said, "*Only I can help you,*"[20] She was speaking the absolute, literal truth. When She said, "*Make it known to the Holy Father that **I still await the Consecration of Russia** to My Immaculate Heart. **Without this Consecration, Russia cannot be converted, nor can the world have***

---

15   John 8:43-44, 46-47, emphasis added.

16   John 18:37. "For this was I born, and for this came I into the world; that I should give testimony to the truth."

17   John 8:32. "And you shall know the truth: and the truth shall make you free."

18   2 Corinthians 11:14.

19   Apparition of July 13, 1917.

20   Ibid.

peace,"[21] She was spelling out in the plainest possible language what we need to know and do in order to avoid the annihilation of nations and the enslavement of mankind to the devil under the Masonic New World Order.

We must not let ourselves be deceived about Our Lady's Message, and we must not deceive ourselves.

"Charity Rejoiceth in the Truth"

There is a hierarchy of the virtues, an order ranking each of the virtues in its relation to the others. Charity is the greatest virtue of all, as St. Paul tells us, but he also points out that charity *rejoices in the truth*.[22] In fact, unless we first love the truth, we cannot really and properly love God or our neighbor, or even ourselves.

Now, certainly there can be a false zeal for the truth which is full of pride and which lacks charity, but nevertheless we can never have true charity without love for truth. And the virtue of loving the truth is getting more and more lost in our time. We must understand the relationship between truth and charity.

Simply put, knowledge and truth must come before love. We cannot love something *at all* unless we first know it, at least in some way. And we cannot love something or someone *properly* so long as we misunderstand it or him.

To love someone is to will the good to that person. But we cannot *will* the good if we do not *know* what the good is. And we cannot properly will the good *to our neighbor* if we have a wrong idea of what is good *for him*.

If we misunderstand what is truly *good* for him, then despite all of our good will, we cannot love him properly. Even in regard to God, we cannot *love* Him properly (if at all) if we do not know some *truth* about Him.

Some people criticize me for being (as they would say) disloyal to the Holy Father or to the Holy See or to the Secretary of State.

---

21   Reported in the Italian bishops' publication, *Il pellegrinaggio delle meraviglie*, 1960, p. 440. *Cf.* Frère Michel, *The Whole Truth About Fatima*, Vol. III, 2nd edition (Buffalo: Immaculate Heart Publications, 2001), p. 327. Emphasis added.

22   1 Corinthians 13:6, 13.

Cardinal Bertone himself has accused me and my associates[23] of hating him[24] simply because I have urged him to act for his own good, and for the good of the many souls who depend on the Church's obedience to Our Lady of Fatima.

Contrary to what these people think, I do love the Pope. I dare say that I love him more than most, if not all, of his counselors do. Frankly, too, I think that I am showing more love for Cardinal Bertone than he is showing for himself.

I don't say this flippantly. I don't say it to brag about myself either, but if I am accused of being hateful, then I'll respond to the charge. It is my love for God and for neighbor that has driven me throughout the past thirty-six years in this work. I know the truth about Fatima, and about what will befall the Pope and bishops and all of us if they don't obey Our Lady of Fatima very soon. How could I justify not speaking out?

Our Obligation to Love the Truth
Regarding the Prophetic Message of Fatima

There are people who are very industrious about physical labor or about getting ahead in life in temporal concerns, but when it comes to seeking the truth, they're a little lazy.

Our lives (and very likely even our souls) depend on our knowing the truth about Our Lady of Fatima's Message. If we have a true love for our neighbor, it will show itself by our application in learning and spreading the truth that we need to know for our true best interests.

It is because there is so little love of truth in the world and in the Church today, that the Message of Fatima is so little known and so poorly understood. It is because there is so little love of truth in the world and in the Church today, that Our Lady's Message has been reduced to silence and, in effect, Our Lady Herself has been rejected.

If there were a greater love for the truth among Catholics today,

---

23   I and others who helped publish *The Secret Still Hidden*, written by Christopher A. Ferrara.

24   See "Response to Cardinal Bertone's False Claims Against the Fatima Center, *The Fatima Crusader*, Issue 90, Winter 2008, pp. 21ff (http://www.fatimacrusader.com/cr90/cr90pg21.pdf). See also *The Fatima Crusader*, Issue 101, Spring 2012, pp. 66ff (http://www.fatimacrusader.com/cr101/cr101pg3.pdf).

we would see many more people seeking out the truth about the Fatima Message, and then defending and promoting it.

But what response has Our Lady of Fatima received? She has not been given the attention that She deserves. We have not acted on Her Message. We have not passed it on. In a word, we have not loved it. We have set the truth aside, because it conflicted with other things that had a higher place in our hearts — *baser* things, such as human respect, and a complacency that doesn't want to be troubled about controversies.

When I say "we" I'm not necessarily talking about every last individual, but I am saying that, in general, by and large, this is the way Catholics have responded to the Message of Fatima.

There is a great silence throughout much of the Church today about the Fatima requests. According to many, it would be disloyal to contradict what Cardinal Bertone has said, or to embarrass or bother him or other churchmen. But the fact is, if we love the truth, we cannot take that attitude.

If you see a child in danger and you can prevent him from hurting himself or from hurting someone else through his lack of knowledge or lack of experience, you have an obligation in charity to tell him about his situation. You have an obligation to say it over and over until you find a way to make that child understand that you're telling him something serious, with major consequences for his safety.

This is the position we are in. All of us who understand Our Lady's Message have this obligation to speak out about it over and over again, to everyone who will listen to us. There is *no more important Message for our time* — there is nothing that compares with the Message of Fatima, both in terms of its completeness in addressing our present needs, and in terms of the seriousness of the consequences of neglecting it.

Pope John Paul II explained the whole Message of Fatima as a response of Our Heavenly Mother's love. Why did She come to Fatima? The Holy Father answers this question with another question:

"Can the Mother, Who with all the force of the love that She fosters in the Holy Spirit and Who desires everyone's salvation, can She remain silent when She sees the very foundations of Her children's salvation undermined? No, She cannot remain silent."[25]

When this Mother saw Her children in danger, She could not remain silent. The eternal salvation of Her children's souls was at stake, and this remains the case today. Even one soul would be enough to speak out for, but we're talking about millions or billions of souls, whose salvation will depend ultimately on our response to Our Lady's Message:

"If what I say to you is done, many souls will be saved...."

Truth Before Personal Loyalties

Fatima is opposed by people who claim to love Our Lady. God knows their hearts — I don't pretend to be able to judge them. But I do say that it is impossible to love Our Lady rightly and at the same time to despise the fullness of the truth that She came to give us.

These people say that I am against the Pope. How can that be, when I am trying to save the Pope's neck, literally? The Pope was given a message[26] through Sister Lucy[27] by Our Lord Himself, warning that for delaying the execution of His command to consecrate

---

25   Sermon at Fatima, May 13, 1982. *Cf.* Father Paul Kramer, *The Devil's Final Battle*, 2nd Edition (Terryville, Connecticut: The Missionary Association, 2010), pp. 199, 216. Taken from the *L'Osservatore Romano*, May 17, 1982 English edition; *cf.* "13 May: Pope John Paul's Homily at Mass in Fatima", *The Fatima Crusader*, Issue 9-10, Oct. - Dec. 1982, pp. 5-6; at www.fatima.org/crusader/cr09/cr09pg05.asp.

26   Revelation of August 1931 to Sister Lucy (two years and two months after Our Lady's formal request for the Consecration of Russia on June 13, 1929), related to her bishop in a letter of August 29, 1931: "*Make it known to My ministers that given they follow the example of the King of France in delaying the execution of My command, they will likewise follow him into misfortune.*" (Father Joaquin Alonso, *Fatima Ante la Esfinge*, Madrid, "Sol de Fatima" Press, 1979, p. 97.) Five years later, Sister Lucy related more about this same revelation in a 1936 letter to her confessor, Fr. José Gonçalves. After giving the details of Our Lady's formal request for the Consecration in 1929, Lucy added: "Later on, by means of an interior communication, Our Lord complainingly said to me: '*They did not want to heed My request. Like the King of France they will repent and do so, but it will be late. Russia will already have spread her errors throughout the world, causing wars and persecutions of the Church. The Holy Father will have much to suffer!*'" (Father Antonio Martins, *Documentos de Fátima*, Porto, 1976, p. 465.) Both texts cited in Frère Michel de la Sainte Trinité, *The Whole Truth About Fatima*, Vol. II (Buffalo, New York: Immaculate Heart Publications, 1989), pp. 543-544.

27   Lucia dos Santos had been one of the three children to whom Our Lady of Fatima appeared in 1917.

Russia, the Pope would follow the King of France into *disgrazia* (as they say in Italian), into misfortune.

Our Lord referred to King Louis XVI, who was the King of France when the French Revolution broke out in 1789. The king was executed at the guillotine, as if he were a criminal. Similarly, in the Third Secret Vision[28] published by the Vatican in June 2000, we see a Pope being executed. In both cases, Our Lord says, these sufferings come as a result of not obeying. In the case of the King of France, it was due to the 100-year disobedience of not consecrating France to the Sacred Heart of Jesus. In the second case it will be because the popes for a long time (100 years?) have not consecrated Russia.

Since the time when these prophecies were given, no Pope together with the Catholic bishops has consecrated Russia, and no Pope has been executed. We know, therefore, that the prophetic vision of the Third Secret is not about things in the past. These terrible prophecies are coming closer and closer to being realized.

The plain truth of the Fatima Message is that our lives and souls are in the greatest danger. The whole world will be enslaved to a satanic regime (the New World Order [N.W.O.]), and entire

---

28 Cardinal Ratzinger and Archbishop Bertone published on June 26, 2000 a text of Sister Lucy's writings which they claimed was the entire Third Secret. The claim that it was entire has subsequently been proven to be false. However, the text they did publish (which was authentic) is as follows:

"After the two parts which I have already explained, at the left of Our Lady and a little above, we saw an Angel with a flaming sword in his left hand; flashing, it gave out flames that looked as though they would set the world on fire; but they died out in contact with the splendour that Our Lady radiated towards him from her right hand: pointing to the earth with his right hand, the Angel cried out in a loud voice: 'Penance, Penance, Penance!'. And we saw in an immense light that is God: 'something similar to how people appear in a mirror when they pass in front of it' a Bishop dressed in White 'we had the impression that it was the Holy Father'. Other Bishops, Priests, men and women Religious going up a steep mountain, at the top of which there was a big Cross of rough-hewn trunks as of a cork-tree with the bark; before reaching there the Holy Father passed through a big city half in ruins and half trembling with halting step, afflicted with pain and sorrow, he prayed for the souls of the corpses he met on his way; having reached the top of the mountain, on his knees at the foot of the big Cross he was killed by a group of soldiers who fired bullets and arrows at him, and in the same way there died one after another the other Bishops, Priests, men and women Religious, and various lay people of different ranks and positions. Beneath the two arms of the Cross there were two Angels each with a crystal aspersorium in his hand, in which they gathered up the blood of the Martyrs and with it sprinkled the souls that were making their way to God." (Congregation for the Doctrine of the Faith, *The Message of Fatima*, June 26, 2000, http://www.vatican. va/roman_curia/congregations/cfaith/documents/rc_con_cfaith_doc_20000626_ message-fatima_en.html)

nations are going to be annihilated,[29] unless we respond to Our Lady of Fatima's requests.

The truth is more important than appearances or personal loyalties. The truth *must* be defended and propagated. We should do it in charity, I agree, and I hope that I do act charitably. God knows, I will be judged for this like everyone else. But we must at all costs, first and foremost, love and defend and promote the truth.

As I have said many times, I don't hate Cardinal Bertone. I pray for him every day. Our love for the truth forces us to publicly oppose Cardinal Bertone because he has taken a public position which is not true. Our defense of the truth is not motivated by personal hatred — not by any means. We have taken our position simply because the truth is a higher good than the deference that we all desire to show to a Vatican official.

We need to have the right attitude about our loyalty to the office and the person of Church officials. Regardless of their rank — the Pope, the Cardinals and Patriarchs, the bishops and priests — there is no authority in the Church that can legitimately deceive the faithful in any way, and especially in a matter that can jeopardize their eternal salvation.

That's exactly what has been going on for the past fifty years, and not just in regard to Fatima. The Faith itself is under attack *from within the Church*, as Our Lady has warned (and as we will discuss further in this book).

Our Obligation to Inform Ourselves and to Defend the Truth

God gave us our intelligence for a reason, and we need to use it. This is why learning the Catechism is so important, because God wants us to know the Faith — each one of us. Our Lord doesn't simply say: "Be baptized, receive the Sacraments, and take as Gospel truth everything that comes out of the mouth of a priest, a bishop, a Cardinal or a Pope!"

Even Andrea Tornielli, a *Vaticanista* at that time attached to the

---

29   Our Lady of Fatima said in Her apparition of July 13, 1917: "*If My requests are heeded, Russia will be converted, and there will be peace; if not, she will spread her errors throughout the world, causing wars and persecutions of the Church. The good will be martyred, the Holy Father will have much to suffer, various nations will be annihilated.*" Frère Michel, *The Whole Truth About Fatima*, Vol. I (Buffalo: Immaculate Heart Publications, 1989), p.182.

secular newspaper *Il Giornale*, who spoke at our 2011 *Consecration Now!* Conference, said: "If the Pope were to preach heresy — which is conceivable, according to Church doctrine — then we must not follow him in that."[30] Well, how are we going to know if the Pope is preaching heresy unless we first examine what he says and try to understand it? On the other hand, there is nothing in the Catholic Faith, or in Catholic practices and Tradition, or in Catholic theology that would justify such a shameful attitude as "The Pope said or did that or this scandalous thing but you must just accept it and not speak out against it!"

We have to do some intellectual work, we have to think for ourselves, we have to *seek the truth*! Intellectual sloth is a vice, even when it is dressed up in words like "obedience" and "loyalty" to salve our consciences.

There is no excuse for the way so many Catholics have willfully blinded themselves to the truth of the Message of Fatima. Our Lady spoke in the simplest terms imaginable: "*If My requests are heeded, Russia will be converted, and there will be peace.*"[31] From that moment to the present time, there has been no conversion of Russia and no peace in the world, but along comes the Vatican Secretary of State saying: "The consecration was done in 1984. Sorry you missed it. There was no mention of Russia and no participation of all the bishops,[32] but that was it." And people respond,

30   Reported in *The Fatima Crusader*, Issue 101, p. 68 (http://www.fatimacrusader.com/cr101/cr101pg3.pdf).

31   Apparition of July 13, 1917.

32   Our Lady made Her formal request for the Consecration of Russia in an apparition in Sister Lucy's convent chapel in Tuy, Spain on June 13, 1929. Lucy recounted Our Lady's request in this handwritten journal entry, dated November 6 of the same year: "*Our Lady said, 'The moment has come in which God asks of the Holy Father to make, and to command that in union with him and at the same time, all the bishops of the world make the consecration of Russia to My Immaculate Heart,' promising to convert it because of this day of prayer and worldwide reparation.*" (Father Antonio Martins, *Fatima e o Coraçao de Maria*, Sao Paulo, Loyola Publications, 1984, pp. 78-79; cited by Frère Michel, *The Whole Truth About Fatima*, Vol. II, p. 555.)
      Regarding the participation of all the bishops, Sister Lucy clarified for Pope John Paul II through his emissary Archbishop Santo Portalupi (the Apostolic Nuncio to Lisbon), along with the Nuncio's personal advisor, Dr. Francisco Lacerda, and Bishop do Amaral of Leiria, in a meeting in her convent parlor on March 21, 1982 (the details of which were related to Father Pierre Caillon, the head of the Blue Army in France, by Dr. Lacerda): "*So that the bishops of the world be united to the Pope in this Consecration of Russia to the Immaculate Heart of Mary, the Pope must **either convoke all the bishops** to Rome, or to another place — to Tuy for example — **or else order the bishops of the entire world to organize, each in his own cathedral,***

"OK, thanks, I can go to sleep again."

a solemn and public ceremony of Reparation and of Consecration of Russia to the Sacred Hearts of Jesus and Mary." (Pierre Caillon, *La Consecration de la Russie aux Tres Saints Coeurs de Jesus et de Marie*, ed Tequi, 1983, p. 31, emphasis added. Cited by Frère François de Marie des Anges, *Fatima: Tragedy and Triumph*, Buffalo, New York, Immaculate Heart Publications, 1994, p. 156.)

This information was not transmitted accurately to the Holy Father. Two months later, on May 13, 1982, John Paul II made a solemn consecration, not of Russia, but of the world, and without having ordered the Catholic bishops of the world to join him. Afterward, when asked about the significance of this attempt in light of the Fatima request, Sister Lucy replied, *"The Consecration of Russia, that which Our Lady has requested, has not yet been done."* (Letter of August 11, 1982, to her cousin, Maria do Fetal, published by Fr. Pierre Caillon in *La Consecration de la Russie aux Tres Saints Coeurs de Jesus et de Marie*, pp. 45-46; cited by Frère François, *Fatima: Tragedy and Truimph*, p. 164.)

The Pope sent Archbishop Portalupi to interview Sister Lucy again the following year, in preparation for another consecration ceremony to take place in 1984. This interview took place on March 19, 1983. Doctor Lacerda was again invited to attend, as was also Father Messias Coelho (a Portuguese Fatima scholar and long-time friend of Sister Lucy). Sister Lucy read aloud to the three this prepared statement: "*In the Act of offering of May 13, 1982, Russia did not appear clearly as the object of the consecration. And each bishop did not organize in his own diocese a public and solemn ceremony of reparation and consecration of Russia. Pope John Paul II has simply renewed the consecration of the world made by Pope Pius XII on October 31, 1942. Of this consecration of the world one may hope for certain good effects, but not the conversion of Russia.*" (Reported by Fr. Pierre Caillon in the monthly periodical *Fidelite Catholique*, B.P. 217-56402, Auray Cedex, France; cited by Frère François, *Fatima: Tragedy and Triumph*, p. 165.)

The Holy Father (apparently unable to overcome resistance within his Curia to a specific Consecration of Russia) went ahead with his plans for making another consecration, but again merely a consecration of the world. This time, however, Pope John Paul II did at least *invite* (not order) the bishops to join him.

On March 22, 1984, three days before this ceremony was to take place, Sister Lucy was visiting with her old friend, Maria Eugenia Pestana. Maria asked, "Then, Lucy, Sunday is the Consecration?" And Lucy replied (having already been presented a copy of the text that the Holy Father would use): *"That consecration cannot have a decisive character. ... Russia does not appear in it as the sole object of the consecration."* (Frère François, *Fatima: Tragedy and Triumph*, pp. 167-168. This reply was reported by Mrs. Pestana in a telephone conversation the next day to Fr. Caillon, who subsequently related the incident to Frère Michel in a letter dated March 30, 1984.)

The ceremony took place as planned, on March 25, 1984, with very few of the world's 3000+ Catholic bishops in attendance. More than a year later, Sister Lucy was interviewed by a representative of the Spanish chapter of the Blue Army, for an article to be published in their official journal, *Sol de Fatima*. Asked if now, after John Paul II's act of 1984, the consecration had at last been done as requested by Our Lady, Lucy replied: "*No. Many bishops attached no importance to this act.*" The questioner urged Sister Lucy, "John Paul II had invited all the bishops to join in the consecration of Russia, which he was going to make at Fatima on May 13, 1982, and which he was to renew at the end of the Holy Year in Rome on March 25, 1984, before the original statue of Our Lady of Fatima. Has he not therefore done what was requested at Tuy?" To this, Sister Lucy replied flatly, "No. *There was no participation of all the bishops and there was no mention of Russia.*" (*Sol de Fatima*, September 1985.)

This kind of sloth is one of the great sins of our age, and it is leading many people to hell.

The love of truth requires that we seek the truth, and embrace the truth. We must also defend and insist upon the truth. We cannot claim that we really love the truth if we do not embrace and defend it. We cannot claim that we really love our fellow men in this world if we do not try to help them acquire what we know to be for their good, what we know to be necessary for their salvation.

We need to have a clear understanding of what our obligations are, in the eyes of God and of Our Lady. Our first obligation in regard to Our Lady of Fatima is to seek and embrace — to love — the truth of Her Message.

The prophecies of Fatima are not opposed to the devotions of Fatima. Now, it shouldn't be necessary to say this. How could they possibly be opposed to one another? It's impossible. But for the past twenty years and more, some unscrupulous men in high positions in the Church have been representing these two aspects of the Message as if they were in opposition.

These men have abused both their authority in the Church and the trust that the faithful have instinctively placed in them. We see this with the letter that came from the Vatican in July 1988 — apparently from Cardinal Casaroli — saying that we must all think and say that the Consecration of Russia is done.

Holy obedience can never demand of us that we tell a lie. Whether it's a priest, a bishop, a Cardinal, or the Pope, no one can command you to tell a lie. They can, of course, pronounce that order, but they don't have the authority to issue any such real order.

I have no problem of conscience in contradicting a Cardinal, even the Vatican Secretary of State, if I know that what he's saying is false. Everyone else should have the same conviction and the same ease of decision, but for some reason that is not the case. Most people seem to think that — out of some distorted view of loyalty or obedience or humility — they have to go along with a falsehood. This is not of God. This is of the devil.

Now, someone might say that you have to be sure of yourself before you publicly resist a prelate of the Church, and yes, you do have to be sure of yourself. It's similar to what St. Thomas says[33] about making any public defense of the Faith against public attacks against the Faith. He points out that only someone who is well-versed in theological studies should contend publicly in defense of the Faith, such as in a debate with a non-believer, because if a person is not capable of doing the job properly, he might make the Faith look as if it does not have a satisfactory explanation.

But the converse of that is also true. For those who *do have* the training and knowledge and ability to defend the Faith publicly, there is an *obligation* to do so. And St. Thomas points this out as well, quoting St. Gregory the Great:

> "Just as thoughtless speech gives rise to error, so does an indiscreet silence leave those in error who might have been instructed."[34]

Even those who may not be qualified to represent the Faith in the public forum should still defend the truth in private conversation to the extent that they can.

Now, I can tell you that I'm not relying on any special knowledge that I learned anywhere in my entire course of doctoral studies in sacred theology, when I take this position. This is a matter that even children can understand. We cannot go along with the lies that are being propagated against the Message of Fatima, no matter where those lies come from.

To the extent that the Pope, the bishops, and the priests are for Christ, then that's where our loyalty should be. Much of the time they're all lined up with the Faith, but sometimes they're not. In that case, you have to choose between conflicting loyalties. What should our choice be? First, Christ and the Truth. Christ identifies Himself as the Truth, and that is where our first loyalty has to be.

The Proper Consecration of Russia Will End All Wars

I have taken it upon myself to defend the truth of the Message of Fatima, with a full-time apostolate dedicated entirely to promoting

---

33   St. Thomas Aquinas, *Summa Theologica*, II-II, Q. 10, A. 7.

34   Pope St. Gregory the Great, *Liber Regulae Pastoralis*, ii, 4.

and defending this Message. But many other priests are purposely undermining The Fatima Center's efforts, saying: "Don't listen to Father Gruner. He's disobedient. Don't even read *The Fatima Crusader*. Put it in the garbage."

Father Robert Fox was asked by someone in the Vatican to start his own Fatima apostolate, and he "dutifully" began announcing far and wide that the Consecration is done, and that people should not listen to Father Gruner. We replied in detail to Fr. Fox's claims, in an article titled "Father Fox's Modernist Assault on Fatima" by Christopher Ferrara.[35] It is an important article, and I encourage anyone who is wavering about these issues to read it.

We also have a videotape of an interview with Father Fox in which he was asked: "Has the Consecration of Russia been done?" He replied: "Yes it has." But later, at the end of the interview, he was asked: "Are you worried about anything?" And Father Fox replied: "Yes. I'm worried about war."

Now, here's a man who spent the final twenty years of his life promoting the idea that the Consecration of Russia has been done, and at the same time he tells us that he fears there will be another terrible war — in fact, according to him there will always be war.

But Our Lady of Fatima said that a period of peace will be given to mankind when Russia is properly consecrated to Her Immaculate Heart!

Father Stefano Gobbi of the Marian Movement of Priests asked me privately, back in 1989, when Father Fox was on the warpath about the Consecration being done: "Is Father Fox trying to call the Blessed Virgin a liar?"

Maybe Father Fox didn't intend his statement to come across that way, but, in fact, that is exactly what he was doing, by saying on the one hand: "The Consecration is done," and on the other hand: "We're always going to have war."

Well, you can't have it both ways. The truth is the truth, and the first principle of truth is the principle of non-contradiction. You can't have Our Lady promising a period of peace as soon as Her requests

---

35   This lengthy article (published as a 28-page booklet available from The Fatima Center, see address on page ii) is presented on the web in three parts, starting at http://www.fatima.org/news/newsviews/062504frfox1.asp

are heeded, and then claim that we are always going to be in fear
of more wars, even when Our Lady's requests have been granted,
without calling Her a liar. God have mercy on him.

We Must Not Deceive Ourselves

I don't mean to single out Fr. Fox or Cardinals Casaroli,
Sodano and Bertone as if they were the only churchmen doing
these things. This has been the program virtually from top to
bottom among too many of the clergy for the past 25 years,
starting from the Vatican Secretariat of State and enforced down
to the last Catholic parish or diocesan school or newspaper. It's a
blasphemous campaign to distort and misrepresent the Message of
Fatima, or at the very least to silence those who try to make the true
Message known.

They use all the nefarious tactics of a secret society to do this,
but the Church is not a secret society. As Pope Leo XIII said in his
encyclical on Christian philosophy, God is not only true, but *truth
itself*. Therefore the Church has nothing to fear from the truth. On
the contrary, it is only by seeking and embracing and defending and
insisting on the truth that we will preserve our society and even our
own souls:

> "The only-begotten Son of the Eternal Father, who came
> on earth to bring salvation and the light of divine wisdom to
> men, conferred a great and wonderful blessing on the world
> when, about to ascend again into Heaven, He commanded
> the Apostles to go and teach all nations, and left the Church
> which He had founded to be the common and supreme
> teacher of the peoples. For men whom the truth had set free
> were to be *preserved by the truth*."[36]

We have no hope except in the truth!

I've been forced to reflect over and over again upon the words
that Pope Benedict used when he went to Fatima on May 13, 2010:

> "He *deceives himself* who thinks that the prophetic

---

36   Pope Leo XIII, Encyclical Letter *Aeterni Patris*, "On the Restoration of Christian
Philosophy," 1879, §1, 5.

mission of Fatima is concluded."[37]

Now, we all have to avoid passing judgment on others. The truth, as I said, is fundamental; yet what is clear to one person is not necessarily clear to all. We cannot presume that a person is of bad will, simply on the basis that he doesn't agree with us. Only Our Lord knows the hearts of men.

Nevertheless, Pope Benedict XVI could say without reservation before 500,000 people at Fatima, that the churchmen who have spent so much time and energy trying to propagate this great lie, claiming that "the events to which the third part of the 'secret' of Fatima refers now seem part of the past,"[38] *have deceived themselves* if they actually believe that lie! The truth of the Message and of our situation is so plain, he says, that only by willfully shutting out the truth could you believe such a lie.

And this goes, too, for all the people who take in this lie for the sake of whatever false notions of "obedience" or loyalty or

---

37 http://www.vatican.va/holy_father/benedict_xvi/homilies/2010/documents/hf_ben-xvi_hom_20100513_fatima_ en.html. The Vatican's English translation weakened the Pope's statement dramatically, to read: "We would be mistaken [instead of "He deceives himself"] to think that…" But the Pope's Italian original was very strong and quite clear: "Si illuderebbe chi pensasse che la missione profetica di Fatima sia conclusa."

38 This is the expression of Cardinal Angelo Sodano in his "Announcement" of May 13, 2000 regarding the long-overdue publication of the Third Secret. In the publication of the Third Secret Vision on June 26, 2000, Archbishop Bertone likewise insisted that Our Lady of Fatima's warnings and requests no longer pertain to our times: "The decision of His Holiness Pope John Paul II to make public the third part of the 'secret' of Fatima brings to an end a period of history marked by tragic human lust for power and evil…." *Cf.* Congregation for the Doctrine of the Faith, *The Message of Fatima*, June 26, 2000; http://www.vatican.va/roman_curia/congregations/cfaith/documents/rc_con_cfaith_doc_20000626_message-fatima_en.html
    Bertone persisted in these patent falsehoods even more virulently after his elevation to the Cardinalate. In his 2007 book, *The Last Visionary of Fatima*, he claimed: "The media have doggedly refused to resign themselves to the fact that the prophecy is no longer open to the future, but refers to something that now belongs to the past." (From p. 67 of the English edition, published in 2008.) Again in 2010, the Cardinal fumed in his new edition of the same book but with an altered title, *The Last Secret of Fatima:* "The journalistic obstinacy consists of not allowing themselves to accept that the prophecy has been realized in the past, in the indicated event [*i.e.*, in the assassination attempt on the Pope in 1981]."
    This latter edition of Cardinal Bertone's book was published on May 4, 2010 — scarcely one week before Pope Benedict's words at Fatima on May 13 quoted above regarding those who so foolishly *deceive themselves* that Our Lady's Message concerns only the past. Thus the Pope's words were rightly construed as a pointed and public rebuke of Cardinal Bertone himself.

submission they might have. He didn't say, 'you would be mistaken' — he said that you are *deceiving yourself* if you think this.

There are people who disagree with what I'm saying, who claim to be more Catholic than I am, who claim to be more loyal and more faithful to the Church than I am, who claim to love the Pope more than I do, and God knows if they do or if they don't. But the Holy Father himself said that these people are *deceiving themselves* about the Message of Fatima.

They are *deceiving themselves* when they say that Our Lady's request for the Consecration of Russia has been satisfied. They *deceive themselves* when they say the whole Third Secret has been released. They *deceive themselves* when they say that the horrifying prophecies of the Third Secret are part of the past. And this lie will cost millions, or quite possibly *billions*, of people their lives and their eternal salvation if we don't break through this deception in time.

A real love of the truth necessarily means *defending* the truth, and denouncing untrustworthy false teachers who are misleading the faithful. It is not disobedient or wrongly "divisive" to stand up for the truth in the face of these lies. *It is the lies themselves that are divisive.* To go along with these deceptions, to go along with these lies, is dangerous. If left to prevail, these lies are bound to kill millions and millions of souls. These lies are from the father of lies — the devil. These lies must be unmasked. The liars must be stopped before they destroy the whole world.

Chapter 2

The Dogmas of the Faith Can Never Fail

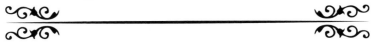

Re-Orienting Ourselves in a Time of Diabolic Disorientation

Even in times of great confusion (such as our own post-Vatican II era), we Roman Catholics must know with certitude and be able to agree with other faithful Catholics to the truth of some very basic things:

What is the purpose of life? What is the ultimate measure of real success in life?

Going to Heaven!

What must we do to save our souls and go to Heaven?

We must know, love, and serve God in this life as faithful Catholics!

How do we live as faithful Catholics?

It is necessary...

- **To be united to the Catholic Church by Baptism (or at least by the desire and intention to be baptized at our soonest fitting opportunity);**[39]

---

[39] The Council of Trent — Session 6, Chapter 4:

"By which words a description of the Justification of the impious is indicated, — as being a translation, from that state wherein man is born a child of the first Adam, to the state of grace and of the adoption of the sons of God (Romans 8:15) through the second Adam, Jesus Christ, our Saviour. And this translation, since the promulgation of the Gospel, cannot be effected except through the laver of regeneration (Canon 5, Session 5), or the desire thereof, as it is written: Unless a man be born again of water and the Holy Ghost, he cannot enter into the kingdom of God (John 3:5)."

The Council of Trent — Session 7:

"If anyone shall say that the Sacraments of the New Law are not necessary for salvation, but are superfluous, and that although all are not necessary for every individual, without them, or without at least the desire for them, through faith alone men obtain from God the grace of justification; let him be anathema." (DZ 847)

- To persevere in the state of sanctifying grace by avoiding grave (i.e. mortal) sin, or to recover sanctifying grace as soon as possible and especially before our death through a sacramental Confession or an Act of Perfect Contrition;
- To persevere as members of the Catholic Church by avoiding to fall into heresy, apostasy, and schism (each of which separates a person from the Church).

But how can we know what the Catholic Faith truly is (and thus avoid falling into heresy), when today so many priests and bishops contradict each other about what we are to believe?

We can be certain that our beliefs conform to the true Catholic Faith when we have for our guides the dogmatic definitions of the Church — that is, the solemn, infallible expressions of the Church's teachings, which can never fail to show us the precise truth as revealed by God.

Our Eternal Salvation Should Be Our First Concern

Our most important concern in this life should be our eternal salvation. As Our Lord said,

"What shall it profit a man, if he gain the whole world, and suffer the loss of his soul?"[40]

A person may think that by conforming himself to the demands of the New World Order or of the coming One-World Religion, he will be able to have peace with the powers-that-be, and to preserve some measure of prosperity in this world. In fact, if he pays the price of denying the true Faith (i.e. the Catholic Faith) or if he lives contrary to the law of Jesus Christ, then even if he manages to preserve his life or his possessions for some time, he will profit nothing. Instead, he will burn in hell for all eternity for his infidelity to the teachings and commandments of Jesus Christ (unless he recovers the state of grace before he dies by the means expressed above).

---

40   Mark 8:36.

The Basis of Our Salvation ... *the Catholic Faith!*

We saw above that Pope John Paul II, in his sermon at Fatima on May 13, 1982, said that the very *foundations* of our salvation are being attacked. He asked,

> "Can the Mother, Who with all the force of the love that She fosters in the Holy Spirit and Who desires everyone's salvation, can She remain silent when She sees *the very foundations* of Her children's salvation undermined?"

The Pope then answered his own question: "No, She cannot remain silent." This, he says, is why Our Lady came to Fatima — to warn us of hidden dangers *undermining* our salvation.

What did the Pope mean when he spoke of the *foundations* of our salvation? What is it that serves as the basis of all our efforts to save our souls? The first basis is the *Catholic Faith*. We know this from the Athanasian Creed, which says:

> "Whosoever wishes to be saved, *needs above all to hold the Catholic Faith*; unless each one preserves this Faith whole and inviolate, he will without a doubt perish eternally."[41]

Now, it should be obvious that one cannot hold the Catholic Faith that is necessary for salvation without belonging to the Catholic Church, which transmits that faith and the grace of the Sacraments that sustain faith. That is why, chief among the Church's own dogmatic definitions is the repeated definition of the revealed truth that outside of the Catholic Church there is no salvation:

> "There is but one universal Church of the faithful, outside which no one at all is saved."[42]

> "We declare, say, define, and pronounce that it is absolutely necessary for the salvation of every human

---

41   Dz. 39, D.S. 75, emphasis added. ("Dz." refers to the compendium of Creeds and Definitions assembled by the 19th Century German theologian Heinrich Denzinger. "D.S." refers to an enlarged edition of the Denzinger text made by Adolf Schönmetzer, S.J., known as the "Denzinger-Schönmetzer" text.)

42   Pope Innocent III, Fourth Lateran Council (1215 A.D.). Dz. 430, D.S. 802.

creature to be subject to the Roman Pontiff."[43]

"The most Holy Roman Church firmly believes, professes and preaches that none of those existing outside the Catholic Church, not only pagans, but also Jews and heretics and schismatics, can have a share in life eternal; but that they will go into the eternal fire which was prepared for the devil and his angels, unless before death they are joined with Her; and that so important is the unity of this ecclesiastical body that only those remaining within this unity can profit by the sacraments of the Church unto salvation, and they alone can receive an eternal recompense for their fasts, their almsgivings, their other works of Christian piety and the duties of a Christian soldier. No one, let his almsgiving be as great as it may, no one, even if he pour out his blood for the Name of Christ, can be saved, unless he remain within the bosom and the unity of the Catholic Church."[44]

Notice a key phrase in the last infallible dogmatic definition, by Pope Eugene IV: "unless before death they are joined with Her." This allows for the possibility that some souls are joined to the Church before death without having achieved formal membership because, as we see in the case of those called catechumens, they earnestly desired baptism and membership in the Church but were prevented from achieving it through no fault of their own (a fatal accident, for example).

Today, of course, we see various gestures and initiatives under the label "ecumenism" or "ecumenical movement." But "ecumenism" is not an infallible dogma of the faith; it is only a pastoral program whose results are clearly not what was intended: Christian unity. On the contrary, after about fifty years of "ecumenism," the Protestant sects are further than ever from unity with the Catholic Church. And there is no Christian unity without unity in the one true Church that Christ established, outside of which there is no salvation. That is why Pope Pius XI condemned Protestant-inspired ecumenical gatherings in the 1920s, warning the Catholic bishops not to allow Catholic

---

43   Pope Boniface VIII, the Bull *Unam Sanctam* (1302 A.D.). Dz. 469, D.S. 875.

44   Pope Eugene IV, the Bull *Cantate Domino* (1442 A.D.). Dz. 714, D.S. 1351.

participation in them:

> "So, Venerable Brethren, it is clear why this Apostolic See has never allowed its subjects to take part in the assemblies of non-Catholics: *for the union of Christians can only be promoted by promoting the return to the one true Church of Christ of those who are separated from it,* for in the past they have unhappily left it."[45]

Whatever one thinks of the "Catholic ecumenism" that began after Vatican II, it is not a dogma of the Faith and does not change the dogma of the Faith that outside the Catholic Church there is no salvation.

So the basis, the foundation, of our salvation is the *supernatural virtue of faith* infused in our souls at our Baptism, by which we profess the *Catholic Faith, whole and inviolate*. And the faith of Catholics, as John Paul II told us at Fatima, is being *undermined* by hidden dangers.

The Pope speaks not just of an open, frontal attack by the Church's known enemies, but especially of the snares laid by hidden enemies — of the danger of wolves in sheep's clothing, who would destroy the Church from within.

A heresy preached by a "Catholic" priest or bishop, *as if it were part of the Catholic Faith*, is much more dangerous than any heresy preached by a Protestant minister, or by some other open heretic or apostate or other nonbeliever. And wherever the Faith is under attack and in danger of not being preserved in this or that place, the salvation of souls is being undermined — even if it be in your own parish pews.

The Catholic Rule of Faith

Each of us has the supreme obligation, before all other duties, to preserve our faith — from the moment of our Baptism until the moment we die. We won't have the virtue of faith any more in Heaven, because there we will know God and His Truth directly because we will see God face-to-face. But until that moment, we must keep the Faith, as Saint Paul did:

---

45   *Mortalium animos* (1928 A.D.), n. 10. See also, Dz. 2199, D.S. 3683.

"I have fought a good fight, I have finished my course, I have kept the faith."[46]

Anyone who is not Catholic doesn't really have what the Church teaches is the supernatural virtue of faith, because true faith empowers us to believe *everything* that God teaches. A heretic may believe many things that the Catholic Church teaches, but if his belief were truly *faith*, he would accept *everything* that God teaches through the Catholic Church — *His* Church.

Some good Catholics may be confused about the Faith, and may even misunderstand parts of it to the point of believing things that are contrary to the Faith. But these good Catholics would immediately accept the true teaching of the Church as soon as they are corrected and realize what the Church actually teaches.

Non-Catholics, on the other hand, generally speaking, knowingly reject one or more teachings of the Catholic Church. And by rejecting any single article of Faith, a heretic shows that he holds everything which he believes, only as a matter of his own *opinion*, and not by faith. By faith, we believe all that God has revealed, on the simple basis of *God's own truthfulness and authority*. We don't sit in judgment as our own authority, deciding which Christian teachings we will believe and which ones we won't believe.

As Pope Leo XIII explains,

"Such is the nature of faith that nothing can be more absurd than to accept some things and to reject others. ... He who dissents even in one point from divinely revealed truth, absolutely rejects all faith, since he thereby refuses to honor God as the supreme truth and the formal motive of faith. ... They, who take from Christian doctrine what they please, depend on their own judgments, not on faith."[47]

St. Thomas Aquinas also explains this very clearly:

"[W]hoever does not adhere, as to an infallible and divine rule, to the teaching of the Church, ... has not the habit [virtue] of faith, but holds [accepts as true] that which

---

46   2 Timothy 4:7.

47   Pope Leo XIII, encyclical *Satis Cognitum*, "On the Unity of the Church," 1896, §9.

is of faith otherwise than by faith. ... [I]t is evident that a heretic who obstinately disbelieves one article of faith, is not prepared to follow the teaching of the Church in all things.... Therefore it is clear that such a heretic with regard to one article has no faith in the other articles, but only a kind of opinion in accordance with his own will."[48]

To Mix the Faith with Errors Is to *Lose* the Faith!

Our faith is the basis of our friendship with God. As St. Paul says,

"Without faith it is impossible to please God."[49]

St. Paul speaks, of course, of the supernatural habit (also known as the virtue) of faith, by which a person believes *all* that he knows that God has revealed.

The virtue of faith is that habitual acceptance as true, by one's mind, of all that God has revealed to mankind in the sacred Deposit of Revelation.

God has transmitted this Deposit by means of the Holy Bible and by Sacred Tradition. A person who has the Faith believes explicitly all he knows of the Bible and of Sacred Tradition and, furthermore, he is disposed to accept as true anything else that is in the Sacred Deposit once he becomes aware that that article of Faith is in the Sacred Deposit or once it is taught as coming from God and thus true — by the Catholic Church's Extraordinary Magisterium.

One believes all the Deposit of the Faith because it is God Who reveals it. God cannot be mistaken since He is All Knowing. God cannot lie to us since God is **All Holy**. Thus, God Who cannot lie and Who cannot be deceived or mistaken, must be telling us the truth when He tells us something. Thus, I believe whatever it is He tells me.

But God, Who is the author of our reason, cannot reveal something as true which our reason proves is false. Thus, there is no contradiction between true faith and true reason.

---

48 St. Thomas Aquinas, *Summa Theologica*, II-II, Q. 5, A. 3.

49 Hebrews 11:6.

There are many liars ever abroad who claim that God has revealed something to them. Witness the thousands of contradictory claims of various Protestant churches. Even among the ancient religions of Hinduism, Buddhism, etc. there are contradictions. Similarly, the modern-day Jews contradict other Jews living today. Thus, God knows that mankind needs clear proof that it is He Himself that is speaking.

Thus, God proves it is Himself by miracles — proving He Who is almighty is speaking — and clear-cut prophecies and predictions that become realized — proving that He Who is all knowing, knowing even future events, is speaking.

God has proven over and over again by miracles and prophecies that the Catholic Church is the same one and only Church that was founded by Jesus Christ. The Church itself teaches how we know what exactly the Church all over the world, for all ages and times, has taught is explicitly revealed by God.

In other words, St. Paul speaks of *true* faith — *the* true Faith, our *Catholic Faith*. As St. Alphonsus says,

> "When we say that faith is necessary for the remission of sins, we mean to speak of the *Catholic* faith, not heretical faith. Without the habit of this faith, no man is justified."[50]

Our obligation to safeguard our faith is our highest obligation to God. It is one of the most important of all of our duties in life, to honor and serve Our Lord with a true and correct faith. This is more important than all external good works — more important than our duty to love our neighbor; more important than the respect or deference that we owe to the Pope, or to bishops, priests, family, and friends.

The ancient Galatians had been converted to the Catholic Faith by St. Paul, but then there came some mistaken "extra zealous" preachers (who may have been Jewish Pharisees before they became Christians), telling the Galatians that they couldn't go straight from paganism to Christianity. First, they said, they would have to be circumcised and follow the food-restrictions of the Old Law given

---

50 St. Alphonsus Liguori, *An Exposition and Defense of All the Points of Faith Discussed and Defined by the Council of Trent.*

by Moses.

When St. Paul heard about the Galatians accepting these new teachings, do you suppose he approved of the Galations' submissiveness, and congratulated them for being so pious and zealous? No! He told them that they had *left the Faith*!

Any change to the Revelation given to us by Christ is a deadly *corruption* of it! St. Paul wrote to the Galatians:

> "I wonder that you are so soon *removed from him* that called you into the grace of Christ, unto another gospel; which is not another, only there are some that trouble you, and would pervert the Gospel of Christ. But though we, or *an angel from Heaven*, preach a gospel to you besides that which we have preached to you, *let him be anathema*. As we said before, so now I say again: If anyone preach to you a gospel, besides that which you have received, let him be anathema."[51]

St. Paul tells us not to allow anyone whomsoever, even though he were an angel from Heaven, to lead us away from a pure confession of the Faith, or else we will lose our souls!

Today we have a situation very similar to what the ancient Galatians faced in the scandalous preaching of the "Judaizers." It goes by a different name today (the "New Theology") and it concerns a different set of specific errors, but the problem is the same: false teachers perverting the Gospel of Christ, to all appearances from within the body of the faithful.

We must not listen to the teaching or advice of anyone whomsoever — pastor, bishop, Cardinal, or even the Pope — if that person is proposing a belief that contradicts established Catholic teaching.

What will happen to us if we do not put our love for the truth above our desire to stay in the good graces of those around us (whether our family and friends, or our priests and bishops or the Vatican)? What will happen if we do not love the truth above all the shadowy allurements of this world?

If we are unfaithful to the known truth, then we can come under

---

51 Galatians 1:6-9, emphasis added.

the curse of God that, as St. Paul says, *blinds us* to the truth, so that we can no longer distinguish truth from error:

"And in all seduction of iniquity to them that perish; because they receive not the love of the truth, that they might be saved. *Therefore God shall send them the operation of error, to believe lying:* That all may be judged who have not believed the truth, but have consented to iniquity."[52]

If we are to avoid being taken in by the growing apostasy all around us (which Our Lady of Fatima warned against),[53] we must first recover a correct understanding of the Catholic Faith, and then cling to that known truth with all our might and at any cost. For as St. Paul tells us in his first Epistle to St. Timothy, the Catholic Church is "the house of God, which is the church of the living God, the pillar and ground of the truth." [1 Tim. 3:15]

We Must Be on Our Guard
Against the Errors of Our Day

So many Catholics have been fooled into believing the lies of our

---

52 2 Thessalonians 2:10-11.

53 Father Joseph Schweigl (1894-1964), who was an Austrian Jesuit professor at the Gregorian University and the Russicum in Rome, was sent to Portugal by Pope Pius XII to question Sister Lucy. The interview (which has never been published) took place in the seer's convent in Coimbra on September 2, 1952. Though Father Schweigl was always very scrupulous about maintaining the confidentiality imposed upon him in this mission, he did allow the following remark to one of his colleagues at the Russicum: "I cannot reveal anything of what I learned at Fatima concerning the Third Secret, but I can say that it has two parts: one concerns the Pope. [This part apparently coincides with the Vision of the 'Bishop dressed in White'.] The other, logically — although I must say nothing — would have to be the continuation of the words: 'In Portugal, the dogma of the Faith will always be preserved.'" (This was communicated by that colleague of Father Schweigl in a letter of November 30, 1984 to Frère Michel de la Sainte Trinité. See his work *The Whole Truth About Fatima*, Vol. III, Buffalo, New York, Immaculate Heart Publications, 2001, pp. 337-339, 710.)

Cardinal Luigi Ciappi, who served as personal theologian for five successive Popes through a span of 40 years, tells us more about this latter part of the Third Secret. In 1995, he admitted: "*In the Third Secret it is foretold,* among other things, that *the great apostasy in the Church begins at the top.*" (This was a personal communication to Professor Baumgartner in Salzburg, Austria, published by Fr. Gerard Mura in the periodical *Catholic*, published by the Transalpine Redemptorists, Orkney Isles, Scotland, Great Britain, March 2002, "The Third Secret of Fatima: Has It Been Completely Revealed?"; cited by Christopher Ferrara, *The Secret Still Hidden*, Pound Ridge, New York, Good Counsel Publications, 2008, p. 43. Emphasis added.)

age, which are directly opposed to the Catholic Faith. Amazingly, some of these Catholics (or former Catholics, as the case may be) have become so confused that they seem not even to realize that they have departed from the teaching of the Church.

Sister Lucy recognized this taking place as far back as the early 1970's, when all sorts of reforms and new ideas were being introduced in the name of the Second Vatican Council. Referring to "the disorientation of our time," she lamented:

"It is indeed sad that so many persons let themselves be dominated by the diabolical wave sweeping over the world, and that they are *blinded to the point of being incapable of seeing error*!"[54]

Some people are so careless as to value their Catholic Faith so little and take little or no effort to protect their Catholic Faith that it is no wonder those persons lose the Faith with so little provocation. They put the teaching authority of the Church on the same level as the questionable wisdom of non-Catholic teachers, and then follow their own intuitions and preferences in forming their beliefs. They may call themselves Catholic, but in reality they are like the seed that fell among thorns in Our Lord's parable (Matt. 13:3-8, 18-23; Mark 4:3-20; Luke 8:5-15), having kept the Faith of their Baptism only for a while, until it was choked out by false doctrines, or worldly pursuits, or by the devil himself.

Other Catholics are being led astray by false teachers *within* the Church. These unfortunate people may think that they are on solid ground in following the lead of their priests and bishops and Cardinals, while in actuality they are allowing themselves to be led into heresy or apostasy.

These people are too trusting. St. Paul warned both priests and bishops to be on their guard against false doctrines and bad examples of other priests and bishops when he admonished a group of them as follows:

"Take heed to yourselves, and to the whole flock, wherein the Holy Ghost hath placed you [as] bishops,

---

54   Letter of April 13, 1971, to her nephew, Father José Valinho, a Salesian priest, cited in Frère Michel, *The Whole Truth About Fatima*, Vol. III, p. 753, emphasis added.

to rule the church of God, which he hath purchased with his own blood. I know that, after my departure, ravening wolves will enter in among you, not sparing the flock. And *of your own selves* shall arise men speaking perverse things, to draw away disciples after them.

"Therefore watch, keeping in memory, that for three years I ceased not, with tears to admonish every one of you night and day. And now I commend you to God, and to the word of his grace, who is able to build up, and to give an inheritance among all the sanctified."[55]

So if priests and bishops need to be on their guard, so too do the faithful also have to not follow bad Cardinals, bishops and priests.

Besides, these poor people are *too careless* about actually finding the real truth. As Sister Lucy said, Our Lord forsakes no one, but makes His voice known to those who truly desire to follow Him. If we are separated from Him, it is *we* who have left *Him*:

"Their principal fault is that they have abandoned prayer; thus *they have left God*.... [T]he [true] sheep follow their Pastor who truly knows how to guide them and lead them on the good road."[56]

The Holy Ghost does not leave Himself without some witness to the True Faith in our souls, especially when our faith is endangered. But if a person *invites* error into his thinking and makes only a pretense of looking to the Church's rule of Faith, then such a person may well end up with the beliefs that he himself has chosen, and not the Catholic Faith. In effect, he has said, "I know this is not the way Catholics used to believe or act, but I like these new ideas, and I see a representative of the Catholic Church who is teaching these new ideas (or telling me that I can do these things), so that's good enough for me."

Either way, the damage to these people's faith occurs because

---

55   Acts 20:28-32; emphasis added.

56   Letters of April 4, 1970 and April 13, 1971, cited in Frère Michel, *The Whole Truth About Fatima*, Vol. III, pp. 752-753 (emphasis added).

they haven't given sufficient importance and effort to learning and understanding the real teachings of Jesus Christ and of His Catholic Church. They leave themselves an easy prey for the devil, who wants to rob us of this great treasure of our Catholic Faith, which we need whole and intact in order to be saved.

So much carelessness on the part of Catholics, who leave themselves uninformed and unguarded in the most important concern of their lives, cannot be without serious fault. These people have forgotten that it is a grave matter of sin to deny or even to doubt one *dogma* of the Faith (a doctrine of the Catholic Faith that has been infallibly taught by Jesus Christ through His Catholic Church). A person would be culpable for such a sin if his error is a result of having neglected to study the Church's teachings sufficiently, or if he has been careless about safeguarding his faith against false doctrines.

St. Thomas Aquinas teaches that sins against Faith are among the greatest of all sins. If a person (with sufficient reflection and of deliberate will) denies or even doubts a dogma of the Catholic Faith, and dies unrepentant of this sin, then he will go to hell for all eternity. This is why the devil is so anxious to corrupt the precious light of faith that Our Lord has infused into our souls at our Baptism, and why we must at all costs preserve it *whole and undefiled.*

Our souls are at stake in this battle. The devil is trying to rob us of our pure Catholic Faith by deceiving us with false doctrines. We have to be on our guard against false doctrines, even if they come to us from the mouths of priests and bishops and Cardinals — rather, *especially* if they come from priests and bishops and Cardinals. Sister Lucy lays it on the line:

> "Unfortunately, in religious matters, the people for the most part are ignorant, and follow wherever they are led. Hence the great responsibility of those who have the duty of leading them…. It is painful to see such a great disorientation and in so many persons who occupy places of responsibility….

> "[T]he devil has succeeded in *infiltrating* evil under cover of good, and the *blind are beginning to guide others*, as the Lord tells us in His Gospel, and *souls are letting*

themselves be deceived. ... And the worst is that he [the devil] has succeeded in leading into error and deceiving souls having a heavy responsibility through the place which they occupy.... They are *blind men guiding other blind men....*

"Gladly I sacrifice myself and offer my life to God for peace in His Church, for priests and for all consecrated souls, especially for those who are so deceived and misled! ...

"People must recite the Rosary every day. Our Lady repeated this in all Her apparitions, as if to arm us in advance against these times of diabolical disorientation, so that we would *not allow ourselves to be deceived by false doctrines....*"[57]

The Solemn Definitions Are Our Infallible Guides to the Catholic Faith

God is All Knowing, so He cannot be mistaken about what is true. God is also All Holy, so it is impossible that He would deceive us when He reveals the Deposit of Faith. Therefore, when God (Who cannot be mistaken and Who cannot lie) tells us that something is true, then we know that it is true.

We can have certitude about natural things, like the fact that two plus two equals four, because we can demonstrate and understand these things. But we have even more sure knowledge — in fact, the greatest possible certitude — in the supernatural matters that God has revealed for our belief. Without being able to completely understand them, we nevertheless know, with the certitude of Faith, that the supernatural truths revealed by God and taught by the Catholic Church are absolutely true.

How do we know what it is that God has revealed? We know that what is in the Bible is God's word, and we know that Sacred Tradition has also been revealed by God. But there are some passages in Sacred Scripture, and also some aspects of Sacred Tradition, which to the uninstructed may seem to be unclear or even self-contradictory.

---

57 Letters of Sister Lucy to Dona Maria Teresa da Cunha (April 12, 1970) and to Mother Martins (September 16, 1970), cited in Frère Michel, *The Whole Truth About Fatima*, Vol. III, pp. 754-758, emphasis added.

For this reason, God has appointed an authority in this world to define what He means in Sacred Scripture and Sacred Tradition. This authority is the infallible *Magisterium* of the One, Holy, Catholic and Apostolic Church, founded by Jesus Christ Himself.

We know many of the dogmas of Faith through solemn pronouncements of the *Extraordinary Magisterium,* in which these teachings are precisely and infallibly defined. We also know the dogmas of Faith through the *Ordinary and Universal Magisterium,* which is also infallible and which is seen in the constant, consistent and universal teachings of the Church in all times, in all ages all over the Catholic world.

As we said above, the *dogmas* of our Faith are the teachings that the Church has proposed for our belief *with Her infallible teaching authority.* The word "infallible" means "unable to fail," so we know that all of the *doctrines* (teachings) which have been directly proposed by the Church in this way cannot fail. They are infallibly true, and we must give to them our unconditional belief, *the assent of faith.*

In other words, we believe the dogmas of Faith on the basis of God's own truthfulness *(divine faith),* since we know them to have been revealed by Him. We also believe them by virtue of the Catholic Church's authoritative guarantee that these are part of the pure Revelation which the Catholic Church has received from God *(Catholic faith).* So whether we find these dogmas taught by the Church's Ordinary and Universal Magisterium, or whether we are given solemn and explicit definitions of these teachings by the Church's Extraordinary Magisterium, we can be absolutely certain that these dogmatic teachings are true, and we give to them the assent of *divine and Catholic faith.*

The word *infallible* tells us that these definitions are absolutely true, and we know that truth does not change with times and circumstances. All of the definitions of the Church remain timelessly true forever. These teachings cannot be changed, and they will never cease to be true. The definitions will always infallibly express the truth of the Catholic Faith, in those very same words, understood in the same sense and with the very same interpretation (*"eodem sensu, eademque sententia"*)[58] in which they were originally formulated.

---

58   "Oath Against the Errors of Modernism": Pope St. Pius X, Motu Proprio *Sacrorum*

So *dogmas* are any teachings of faith or morals authoritatively proposed as being "of the Faith" (*de Fide*) by the Church's Magisterium (whether by the Ordinary and Universal Magisterium, or by a solemn definition of the Extraordinary Magisterium). We give the assent of divine and Catholic faith to all of these teachings.

Definitions are precise and infallible expressions of the dogmas of Faith solemnly proposed by the Pope, whether alone or in union with other bishops.

Most importantly, it is by studying these infallible definitions (as gathered together in an organized way, for instance, in the popular Denzinger and Denzinger-Schönmetzer compendiums) that we can readily know exactly what the Church teaches in regard to each of the dogmas of Faith.

We have, for instance, a definition which tells us that there are three Persons in one God. We can be *more* certain of that than of anything which we can know by our senses or intellect alone. We can be *more* certain of the defined teaching than we can be that it's hot outside today, or that two plus two equals four. So if someone comes along — whether it be a Pope, a Cardinal, a bishop, a priest or a lay person — and tells us that there *are not* three Persons in one God, then we can be completely certain that he is wrong. It's as simple as that.

We will *know* that this person is wrong, not because *we* are smarter, but because *God* is right, and God cannot and does not deceive us — nor can we miss His meaning in those solemn definitions.

When we profess our belief in what God has revealed, we are making an act of the supernatural virtue of faith, and we are also obeying the First Vatican Council (1869-1870), which teaches:

"[B]y divine and Catholic faith everything must be believed that is contained in the written word of God or in Tradition, and that is proposed by the Church as a divinely revealed object of belief either in a solemn decree or in Her

---

Antistitum, 1910, Dz. 2145. See also Vatican Council I, Dz. 1800, D.S. 3020.

ordinary, universal teaching."[59]

When Is the Pope Infallible?

Is every statement that a Pope makes, an infallible definition? No. Not at all! We must know that these solemn, formal definitions of the Extraordinary Magisterium always must satisfy several precise conditions.

Most Catholics are aware that papal infallibility is not a constant clairvoyant gift, making the Pope right about everything he says and does. Here is how the dogma of papal infallibility was defined (infallibly) by Blessed Pope Pius IX in 1870, during the First Vatican Council:

> "We ... teach and define that it is a divinely revealed dogma, that the Roman Pontiff, when he speaks *ex cathedra* (that is, when, acting in the office of shepherd and teacher of all Christians, he defines, by virtue of his supreme apostolic authority, doctrine concerning faith or morals to be held by the universal Church), possesses through the divine assistance promised to him in the person of St. Peter, the infallibility with which the divine Redeemer willed his Church to be endowed in defining doctrine concerning faith or morals; and that such definitions of the Roman Pontiff of themselves are irreformable, not because of the agreement of the Church. But if anyone presumes to contradict this Our definition (God forbid that he do so): let him be anathema."[60]

So we see that the Pope's *charism* or gift of infallibility is limited in a number of ways. First of all, it pertains only to matters of *faith* and *morals*. But we could fill libraries with papal writings on subjects other than faith and morals. Obviously, not every statement within all of the Popes' homilies, Encyclical Letters, General Audience discourses, Apostolic Letters and Exhortations, Briefs, Bulls, and speeches is an infallible definition.

---

59   First Vatican Council, Session III, "Dogmatic Constitution Concerning the Catholic Faith", Dz. 1792.

60   Dz. 1839, 1840; D.S. 3073-3075.

Besides, there are two other conditions which must be present in an infallible definition. The Pope must be speaking *ex cathedra* — in the role of his office as the ruler of all Christians, the universal teacher and supreme judge of the Church — not simply as a private theologian, or even as the head of a Roman Congregation or tribunal. He must also pronounce his teaching in such a way as to make clear his *intention to bind in conscience* all Catholics throughout the world and for all future ages.

The Pope will often use certain formulaic expressions to indicate that he is officially addressing the whole Church (*e.g.*, "We declare, define, and pronounce...") and that he is binding every member of the Church in conscience to give an assent of faith to his definition (*e.g.*, "If anyone should deny this, let him be anathema"). Pope Pius IX's 1854 definition of Our Lady's Immaculate Conception is a classic example:

> "We declare, pronounce, and define that the doctrine which holds that the most Blessed Virgin Mary, in the first instant of Her conception, by a singular grace and privilege granted by Almighty God, in view of the merits of Jesus Christ, the Savior of the human race, was preserved free from all stain of original sin, is a doctrine revealed by God and therefore to be believed firmly and constantly by all the faithful.

> "Hence, if anyone shall dare — which God forbid! — to think otherwise than as has been defined by Us, let him know and understand that he is condemned by his own judgment; that he has suffered shipwreck in the faith; that he has separated himself from the unity of the Church; and that, furthermore, by his own action he incurs the penalties established by law if he should dare to express in words or writing or by any other outward means the errors he thinks in his heart."[61]

---

61   Dz. 1641, D.S. 2803.

The Definitions Distinguish Dogma from Open Theological Questions

As the name implies, the *definitions* mark out the *boundaries* dividing the Church's infallible teachings (the dogmas of Faith) from theological questions which are legitimately open to differences of opinion, as well as from outright heresies. The definitions show us precisely where these boundaries are.

Let's look at another very recent example. The Church has always taught that the Blessed Virgin was bodily assumed into Heaven at the end of Her earthly life, but the question of whether or not She *died* has been the subject of a longstanding discussion (divided for the most part between Eastern and Western centers of thought).

When Pope Pius XII solemnly defined the dogma of Our Lady's Assumption (in 1950), he purposely did not bind the Church in regard to the question of whether or not Our Lady had died. The Holy Father basically indicated in his definition, "I'm not addressing that issue here. You are free to believe one way or the other about whether Our Lady suffered death, as your own piety and understanding lead you."

Notice how carefully he phrased his definition so as to leave this point open to debate and discussion:

> "We pronounce, declare, and define it to be a divinely revealed dogma, that the Immaculate Mother of God, the ever Virgin Mary, *having completed the course of Her earthly life*, was assumed body and soul into heavenly glory. Hence if anyone, which God forbid, should dare willfully to deny or to call into doubt that which We have defined, let him know that he has fallen away completely from the divine and Catholic Faith."[62]

We see, then, that the *defined dogmas* of Faith — the teachings *de fide definita* — form a catalogue of Christian doctrines carrying the Church's highest degree of authority and certainty. We find solemn definitions of the dogmas of the Immaculate Conception, the Perpetual Virginity, the Divine Maternity, and the Assumption of the Blessed Virgin; the number and necessity of the Sacraments; the

---

62   Dz. 2333, D.S. 3903, emphasis added.

Real Presence of Our Lord in the Blessed Sacrament; the hierarchical constitution of the Church; Papal Primacy and Infallibility, to name a few of the teachings challenged by Protestants.

We look to the solemn definitions for clear enunciations of the Catholic Faith, with the assurance that these formulations — phrased precisely as they are — carry the Holy Ghost's promised protection from any error. They are infallible, and every Catholic (whether Pope, bishop, priest, or layman — theologian and ditch-digger alike) must conform his beliefs to these infallible norms.

No New Dogmas

The loss of dogma by Catholics is apparently one subject dealt with in the Third Secret of Fatima — in that part of the Third Secret that as of July 2014 the Vatican has not revealed.

To give you the reference, recall the opening words of Our Lady, at the start of the Third Part of the Secret:

"In Portugal, the dogma of the Faith will always be preserved etc."

Many Catholics today (including not only lay persons, but even churchmen) have lost their sense of dogma. They no longer understand that the Church's teachings are a *Deposit* of Faith — that these teachings have been *given to us by God* as an *unchanging* revelation. The Catholic Faith is the same today as it was when St. Peter preached his first sermon, on the first Pentecost Sunday. "Jesus Christ, yesterday, and today; and the same forever." [Heb. 13:8] From the 1st Century to the 21st Century, there have been no new teachings added to the Deposit of Faith, and no original teachings outmoded or "revised."

God does not contradict Himself. The teachings that He has revealed are as true today as they always were and always will be. The Deposit of Faith is also a *closed* body of teachings. General Revelation ended with the death of St. John, Our Lord's last living Apostle. So it is impossible that the Church could ever propose a new doctrine that was unknown to prior Christians, or which in any way contradicts or revises what the Church has previously taught.

But since the end of the Second Vatican Council in 1965, this has appeared to many people to be the case. New notions (especially regarding "ecumenism" and "religious liberty," and the possibility of being saved through the practice of any religion whatsoever) have been passed off in various places in the Church as authentic Catholic doctrine, whereas they are the opposite of what the Church has always taught and are still taught by faithful Catholic priests and bishops today.

Other traditional teachings have come to be questioned by the ignorant or the malicious as well during these same years, reaching to the very foundations of the Christian life and religion — from the natural use of the privileges of marriage, to the belief in Our Lord's Real Presence in the Blessed Sacrament. These novelties appear to be tolerated by Church officials, who may themselves have no real authority if they are truly heretics. Since heretics are cut off from the Church, they cannot hold any office in the Church.

But the First Vatican Council clearly taught that the Church's Magisterium *cannot give us new doctrines*. The Magisterium can only pass on and explain what God has revealed through Sacred Scripture and Tradition:

> "[T]he Roman pontiffs, according to the exigencies of times and circumstances (sometimes assembling ecumenical councils, or asking for the mind of the Church scattered throughout the world, sometimes by particular synods, sometimes using other helps which divine Providence supplied) defined as to be held those things which with the help of God they had recognized as conformable with the Sacred Scriptures and Apostolic traditions. *For the Holy Spirit was not promised to the successors of Peter, that by His revelation they might make known new doctrine*, but that by His assistance they might inviolably keep and faithfully expound the revelation or deposit of faith delivered through the Apostles."[63]

The Deposit of Faith was completed by the revelations of Jesus Christ to the Apostles. After the death of St. John, the last living Apostle, there has not been and will not be any new doctrines of the Catholic

---

63   First Vatican Council, "First Dogmatic Constitution on the Church of Christ," 1870, Dz. 1836, D.S. 3069-3070.

Faith. At various times in its history, the Church has *defined*, with its infallible teaching authority, various parts of the Deposit of Faith as often as has been necessary in order to clarify a Catholic teaching and to condemn the heretical errors of the times. But the Church has never proposed a new doctrine for our belief.

The "new" Church teachings that we have been hearing of during the past fifty years are really *pseudo*-doctrines — false teachings that have the appearance of being approved and proposed by the Church. What makes these false teachings especially deceptive and dangerous is that so many churchmen, including many high-ranking Archbishops and Cardinals, have been taken in by them. But no matter how many (or how high-ranking) are these false teachers, their pseudo-doctrines can easily be seen for what they are. When any such teaching contradicts the Church's *infallibly defined* teaching, then we know that we must continue to believe the defined doctrine, and reject the "new" doctrine.

What God has revealed is timeless and true. What the Church has defined to be dogmas of Faith — at the Council of Jerusalem in 50 A.D., or at the Council of Nicea in 325, or at the Council of Florence in 1445, or at the Council of Trent in 1565, or at the First Vatican Council in 1870 — was not invented at the time of those definitions, but has always been part of God's original Revelation to the Church. The *infallible definition* may have been made at any point in the Church's history, but the teaching itself is as old as the Church.

Teachings of the Ordinary and Universal Magisterium Are Also Unchanging

The teachings of the Ordinary and Universal Magisterium are not proposed to us in the form of definitions, but they are nevertheless clear, and they are infallible. This Ordinary and Universal Magisterium is what most of us go by most of the time. We would have no danger of confusing the widespread heresies of our day with authentic teachings of the Ordinary and Universal Magisterium, so long as we have a proper understanding of the word *universal*.

The world *universal* here is not simply about geographical expansion — how far and wide a belief might be held throughout the Catholic world at a particular time. It is also about *time*. We recognize the dogmas of Faith proposed by the Ordinary and Universal Magisterium because they have been taught both throughout the whole world and *throughout the entire history of the Church*. This is how we know that these teachings are *part of the original Revelation* given by God.

For a teaching to belong to the infallible Ordinary and Universal Magisterium of the Catholic Church, it cannot be, in any way, in contradiction to what the Catholic Church has always taught. This is because (as we saw above) the Church's Magisterium is not given to us by God in order to teach new doctrines, but only to explain what is in the Deposit of the Faith — that is, what is in Sacred Scripture and Sacred Tradition.

It doesn't matter how many people may have fallen for some new teaching, or what rank these people may hold in the Church. If it is a *new* teaching and in any way contrary to what the Church has always and everywhere taught, it is not part of the Christian Revelation. It's not Catholic. It's a *false doctrine*.

A "Living Magisterium"?

Some years ago (in the year 2000) I was invited to address a certain group of priests and seminarians and novices who were in the process of trying to start a new community that claimed to be for traditional Latin-rite priests. The superior wanted the whole group to hear what I had to say about the Church's situation in light of the Message of Fatima.

My visit was to be completely unpublicized. They were concerned about having Rome's approval. They didn't want to be associated with any side of a controversial issue within the Church, so no one outside of this immediate group knew about my visit.

As I've said above, I think that the truth of Our Lady of Fatima's Message demands a very different kind of response than this. The good of souls who look to their priests for guidance in such questions also demands more than a hireling's attitude of self-preservation from priests. We saw Sister Lucy's comment above, too, about the responsibility priests have before God to seek and embrace and defend the truth of Our Lady's Message:

"Unfortunately, in religious matters, the people for the

most part are ignorant, and follow wherever they are led. *Hence the great responsibility of those who have the duty of leading them....*"

It is such a pathetic illusion for priests to think that they will preserve anything by staying under the radar in not learning, defending and promoting the Message of Fatima in all its fullness to the extent that they are able. If we don't stand up and act on the truth of the Fatima Message very quickly, we are all going to lose our necks, beyond our positions and salaries and insurance policies!

But I didn't want to miss any opportunity to speak about Our Lady of Fatima, and especially to a group of priests, who could do so much good for Our Lady's cause. So I went to their community and delivered a presentation to them about the Message of Fatima, and then opened the floor for questions.

I had spoken about the dogma of Faith being under attack even from within the Church, and I had made reference to some examples of Church teachings which were losing acceptance among many "Protestantized" Catholics. One of the seminarians of this group brought that point up again and told me that he, for one, did not believe in what I had said was the Church's teaching. It was enough for him to know that a certain Cardinal had said the opposite. *"I follow the living magisterium,"* this seminarian told me!

I could hardly believe my own eyes and ears. This was a seminarian who was preparing to become a priest to say only the traditional Latin Mass, and who had supposedly had a traditional seminary formation. As best I could tell from the discussion that followed, the superior of the group[64] shared this seminarian's understanding of the Church's Magisterium — basically, that a "magisterial teaching" is whatever happens to be the latest word from Vatican officials, no matter how contradictory this might be to the prior constant and defined teachings of the Church!

Poisonous Words

The notions of a "living Tradition" and a "living Magisterium"

---

64   That community subsequently was canonically suppressed by the ordinary of the diocese where it had been originally set up.

came into the vocabulary of Catholics through the modernist theologian, Fr. Henri de Lubac, S.J., the father of the "New Theology." We can trace de Lubac's ideas to the French philosopher Maurice Blondel, who considered truth to be subjective, more closely related to the will and to experience than to the intellect.

Without an understanding of *objective* truth, it's easy to see why any reference to dogma is impossible in Modernist thinking.

Pope Pius XII warned[65] that the subjectivist philosophy typical of Protestantism and Modernism would be the ruin of Catholic theological training if it were ever to succeed in invading our seminaries. Tragically, the old scholastic philosophy and theology have been supplanted by various brands of Modernism in the vast majority of so-called "Catholic seminaries" throughout the world today. We needed to hear the warning from Our Lady Herself. We needed to hear it in Her own words, in the Third Secret of Fatima. We still need to hear Her own words.

Certainly the Church's Tradition is "alive" in the sense that it is able to apply itself to the particular and unique needs of each passing age. Tradition has a vitality capable of fitting its unchanging principles to the ever-changing problems of the day. You can sense this immediately when you begin reading various council documents. The flavor, if you will, of the Council of Nicaea (combating Arianism) is very different than that of the Council of Florence (concerning the Eastern Schism), which differs from that of the Council of Trent (against Protestant errors) and of the First Vatican Council (condemning modern Liberalism). But each of the councils has been a window to the Church's living but constant Tradition.

Tradition (with a capital "T") and Sacred Scripture are the two sources where we find the Deposit of Faith. This Deposit is the Revelation that God has given to mankind, beginning with the gradual revelations made throughout Old Testament times, and finally completed by Our Lord's instruction to the Apostles and in the teachings of the Apostles during their time on earth. It is fixed now, and will never change. Nothing will ever be added to or lost from the Deposit of Faith in the Church's pure confession of that

---

65   *Cf.* especially his Encyclical Letter *Humani Generis*, "Concerning Some False Opinions Threatening to Undermine the Foundations of Catholic Doctrine," 1950.

Faith, regardless of how many individual Catholics or even whole nations may fall away from it.

We have also discussed above that the Church's Magisterium is not capable of issuing new doctrines or of modifying the traditional teachings in any way. Its function is only to pass on and explain those teachings — to "inviolably keep and faithfully expound the revelation or deposit of faith delivered through the Apostles."

It is the delusion of Pentecostals that they can add an eighth Sacrament to the seven instituted by Our Lord, in their Laying-On of Hands. It is the delusion of Modernists, who hold the Sacraments of Confirmation and Penance in such contempt, that they can do away with any of the Sacraments. It is the delusion of Protestants that they can relax Our Lord's commandments to accommodate the permissiveness of our dissolute modern society, by condoning divorce and remarriage, contraception, abortion, and homosexual "unions."

You can find various changeable and changing doctrines among the Mormons and Jehovah's Witnesses, but never in the Catholic Church's *unchanging* Sacred Scripture, Tradition and true Universal Magisterium![66]

Development of Doctrine

The Church is always working to guide and protect souls of each passing age in regard to the errors of their time. Magisterial teachings always move in the direction of a fuller explanation of the same truths already professed, supplying an increase in precision of the Church's explicit teaching, and never in a new and altered sense of that teaching.

St. Vincent of Lerins (a Father of the Church) explains:

"Let the understanding, then, the knowledge and the wisdom, as well of individuals as of all, as well of one man as of the whole Church, throughout the course of ages and centuries increase and make much and vigorous progress; but yet only in its own kind; that is to say, in the same

---

66   That is, the solemn Extraordinary Magisterium of solemn definitions or the Ordinary and Universal Magisterium — but not every word and speech of the Pope or bishops.

doctrine, in the same sense, and in the same meaning."[67]

So we can trace a legitimate *development* of doctrine, as traditional teachings become more and more explicit throughout the ages, but this is very different from the wrongly proposed theory of *evolution* of doctrine whereby a teaching of earlier times now in modern times can change into a new doctrine — even to the point of contradicting what the Church has always taught!

The Voice of a Loving Mother

All the solemn definitions of the Faith are two-edged swords, so to speak. They cut both ways. It is the very essence of a definition to say not only "This is the true teaching," but also therefore to say, "All the opposing notions are false."

So, whether explicitly or implicitly, all definitions condemn error. All definitions warn mankind that those who would follow the condemned false teachings will lose their souls (unless they convert back before they die), not only by corrupting their faith, but also by cutting themselves off from the Church. We need both of these most precious assets of our mortal life in order to be saved — the true Faith, and our union with the Catholic Church. As we saw above, the solemn definitions typically conclude with an anathema, saying that unless a person were to recover from such errors before his death, he would be cursed, condemned to hell.

This is the kind of plain language that we human beings need in order to avoid losing our souls. It is the clear voice of our Mother, the Church, calling those who have fallen to come out of their errors, and at the same time warning Her faithful children to avoid the snares on their path. Every parent knows what a cruel mistake it would be to shield a child from every potentially upsetting aspect of life, only to have him someday face the "real world" without any understanding of its dangers. What mother would not warn her child that the stove is hot and it will burn the child if he touches it? The Magisterium's office of condemning error is perhaps the most *merciful* and *pastoral* of its roles.

Dr. Romano Amerio expresses very well how distorted is the

---

67   St. Vincent of Lerins, *Commonitorium*, xxiii.

understanding of "mercy" that would desire to see the Church present itself to the world stripped of Her authority to condemn errors:

> "The setting up of the principal of mercy as opposed to severity ignores the fact that in the mind of the Church, *the condemnation of error is itself a work of mercy*, since by pinning down error those laboring under it are *corrected* and others are *preserved from falling* into it."[68]

Dr. Amerio wrote those words as a lament over the tragic miscalculations of the Cardinals, Archbishops, bishops and even at times Popes presiding at the Second Vatican Council. (He had served as one of the "periti," or expert advisors, at the Council, and he witnessed much of the colossal folly of those years first-hand.)

At John XXIII's insistence, the Council avoided not only all anathemas, but even any *mention* of the greatest menace to the safety of the world and the Church — Russian Communism.

A "Pastoral" Council?

By the Pope's decision, the Second Vatican Council purposely refrained from engaging the Church's infallible Extraordinary Magisterium. No solemn definitions of doctrine would be issued (in spite of the desire of a large number of bishops that the Council would define the dogma of Our Lady as Mediatrix of all Graces).

After the close of the Council, Pope Paul VI himself insisted that this disclaimer be appended to the Acts of the Council:

> "Taking conciliar custom into consideration and also the pastoral purpose of the present Council, the sacred Council *defines as binding* on the Church *only those things* in matters of faith and morals *which it shall openly declare to be binding*."[69]

The language is a little bit circular, but nevertheless plain. *Only the definitions* are binding on the faithful. And *there are no definitions!* The only binding teaching found in Vatican II is what has always been taught by the Church before Vatican II.

---

68   Romano Amerio, *Iota Unum: A Study of the Changes in the Catholic Church in the 20th Century*, Sarto House, 1996, p. 80, emphasis added.

69   "Appendix" to the Acts of the Council. Emphasis added.

As Paul VI admitted,

"In view of the pastoral nature of the Council, it avoided any extraordinary statements of dogmas endowed with the note of infallibility...."[70]

Cardinal Ratzinger also made this well-known comment:

"The truth is that this particular Council defined no dogma at all, and deliberately chose to remain on a modest level, as a merely pastoral council...."[71]

Monsignor Brunero Gherardini, the highly respected Professor of Ecclesiology at the Pontifical Lateran University, said of the Second Vatican Council that,

"The doctrines which are proper [unique] to it, ...absolutely cannot be considered as dogmatic because they are deprived of the requisite form for defining and hence of the related *voluntas definiendi* [intention to define]. ... [N]one of its doctrines, unless ascribable to previous conciliar definitions, are infallible or unchangeable, nor are they even binding: he who denies them cannot, for this reason, be called a formal heretic. He, then, who imposes them as infallible and unchangeable would be going contrary to the council itself."[72]

I could go on and on citing other theologians to the same effect, but it would be unnecessary here to do so. Church councils have no more authority than the presiding Pope decides to attribute to them. The many statements (some of them noted above) of both John XXIII and Paul VI (both before and after the Council documents were promulgated), to the effect that they intended "not to issue

---

70   General Audience of January 12, 1966, 6th paragraph; http://www.vatican.va/holy_father/paul_vi/audiences/1966/documents/hf_p-vi_aud_19660112_it.html

71   Cardinal Joseph Ratzinger, Address to the Bishops of Chile, July 13, 1988; http://www.catholicculture.org/culture/library/view.cfm?recnum=3032

72   Brunero Gherardini, *The Ecumenical Vatican Council II: A Much Needed Discussion* (Frigento: Casa Mariana Editrice, 2012), pp. 59-60, cited in Roberto de Mattei, *The Second Vatican Council: An Unwritten Story* (Fitzwilliam, New Hampshire: Loreto Publications, 2012), p. xi.

new solemn dogmatic definitions,"[73] should be sufficient to end the question of the level of authority carried by those documents.

The Infallible Definitions Judge the Orthodoxy of All Non-Infallible Expressions

God has revealed to us the mystery of the Blessed Trinity — three divine Persons in one God, a *defined Catholic dogma*. Without being able to fully grasp this mystery, we nevertheless know that it is true because God has revealed it and the Church has proposed it for our belief with the highest measure of its magisterial authority.

Heaven forbid that it should happen one day that your pastor (or bishop, or even the Pope himself or a Third Vatican Council) announces to you, "We've had it wrong all these years. There are actually *four* divine Persons in God."

Even if such a preposterous thing were to happen, you wouldn't need to wait for the next Pope or the Fourth Vatican Council to set the matter straight. *We already have the definition.*

God could not possibly have told prior generations something that was not true, and that is liable to being updated or corrected in later times. The definitions are irreformable by their very nature, as the First Vatican Council defined, and their truth does not depend upon the continued agreement of Popes, Cardinals, bishops and priests. What was true yesterday cannot cease to be true today or tomorrow. It is impossible.

And yet we have so many Catholics saying about a great number of teachings: "Oh well, that was the teaching *before* Vatican II. The Church doesn't teach that anymore. I'm following the Ordinary and Living Magisterium. The Pope and bishops of our time have made the New Theology of Henri de Lubac and Hans Urs von Balthasar the official theology of the Church today."

It is true that the Popes and bishops of the past half-century have contributed much to the present confusion. But it doesn't matter *who* the mouthpiece is for such doctrinal novelties. If a Pope alone or a council with the Pope are not *defining a dogma of the Faith*, their words must be measured against the infallible yardsticks of the

---

73   Paul VI, General Audience Address of March 8, 1967, 4th paragraph; http://www. vatican.va/holy_father/paul_vi/audiences/1967/documents/hf_p-vi_aud_19670308_ it.html

Church's true Magisterium. If what *anyone* says is contradictory to prior continuous and universal teachings of the Church, or to any of the Church's solemn definitions, then that person is promoting a false teaching.

If it's false, it's false! No human authority can change that — not even the Pope's.

This is why every doctrine must be judged against the infallible definitions. In doubtful cases, we can receive the suspect teachings only with reservations. And in cases of obvious contradiction to defined Catholic dogma, we must adhere to the articles of Faith precisely as they are defined, and avoid the contrary teaching altogether.

Vatican II cannot be a "Super-Council" that overrides all other councils, because no council is a magisterium unto itself, reinventing the Faith of the Church as it will.

Since Vatican II did not exercise its power to define dogma and to anathematize error, everything taught by the Council that had not been previously taught with the Church's infallible Magisterium (whether Extraordinary or Ordinary and Universal), has to be examined in the light of prior teachings, especially the solemn definitions. The infallible Magisterium is the gauge of the usefulness and orthodoxy of Vatican II — not the other way around.

However, what's happening today is that people are attempting to redefine Catholic dogma in light of Vatican II, even against the solemn definitions. Even Cardinal Ratzinger (who was later elected Pope Benedict XVI) admitted the insanity of this situation:

> "The Second Vatican Council has not been treated as a part of the entire living Tradition of the Church, but as *an end of Tradition, a new start from zero*. The truth is that this particular Council defined no dogma at all, and deliberately chose to remain on a modest level, as a merely pastoral council; and *yet many treat it as though it had made itself into a sort of superdogma which takes away the importance of all the rest*."[74]

---

74 Cardinal Joseph Ratzinger, Address to the Bishops of Chile, July 13, 1988, emphasis added. See also footnote 71.

Needless to say, the end product of this mental circus act too often leads people to fall away from the Catholic Faith.

A Duty to Resist

There is a famous maxim attributed to the 5th Century Pope, St. Felix III, about standing up for the truth:

> "Not to oppose error is to approve it; and not to defend truth is to suppress it."

This saying is especially true in regard to opposing doctrinal errors and defending the true Faith — regardless of the source of those errors. Even a Pope may be legitimately resisted if he were to act in a way that is contrary to the Faith or otherwise harmful to the Church.

When the Pope and bishops preach the truth of the Catholic Faith to us, as they have received it from authentic magisterial sources, God expects us to believe them. And when they tell us to do something within the realm of their jurisdiction, He expects us to obey.

But if the Pope tells us to do something contrary to the manifest good of the Church, or to profess a belief in something contrary to the Catholic Faith (such as a fourth Person of the Blessed Trinity), we don't have to obey him. We must "disobey" him — that is, we must resist him, and obey God rather than men, as St. Peter said.[75] Otherwise we make ourselves guilty of a sinful false obedience (or as St. Thomas calls it, indiscreet obedience).[76]

At the turn of the 17th Century, Protestants were slandering the papacy as a sort of despotism. The Pope, in their view, was an absolute monarch whose power was unrestrained by any law. Saint Robert Bellarmine answered this charge, demonstrating that the Pope's authority is by no means unlimited or arbitrary:

> "Just as it is licit to resist the Pontiff that aggresses the body, it is also licit to resist the one who aggresses souls or who disturbs civil order, or above all, who attempts to

---

75   Acts 5:29.

76   St. Thomas Aquinas, *Summa Theologica*, II-II, Q. 104, A. 5, ad 3.

destroy the Church. I say that *it is licit to resist him* by not doing what he orders and by preventing his will from being executed; it is not licit, however, to judge, punish or depose him, since these acts are proper to a superior."[77]

It shouldn't be necessary to belabor this point, but truly there are so many Catholics today who have a dangerous misunderstanding of the papacy. They seem to believe that they are somehow expressing a loyalty to Christ or to the Church by saying such things as, "I'd rather be wrong with the Pope than right without him!" Some foolish, ignorant Catholics have even said to me they would rather follow the Pope and go to hell with him rather than disobey the Pope. There is nothing Catholic about such slogans.

The great 16th Century theologian Francisco Suarez, whom Pope Paul V praised as "the Exceptional and Pious Doctor" (*Doctor Eximius et Pius*), taught:

"If [a Pope] gives an order contrary to right customs [morality], he should not be obeyed; if he attempts to do something manifestly opposed to justice and the common good, it will be lawful to resist him...."[78]

Before Suarez, the eminent medieval theologian Cardinal Juan de Torquemada (who formulated the definitions issued at the Council of Florence) had written on the same subject:

"Were the Pope to command anything against Holy Scriptures, or the articles of faith, or the truth of the sacraments, or the commands of the natural or divine law, he *ought not to be obeyed*, but in such commands he is to be disregarded."[79]

And before Torquemada, St. Thomas Aquinas had demonstrated the right and *duty* of the faithful (including members of the clergy) to publicly correct and even rebuke ecclesiastical superiors whose

77   St. Robert Bellarmine, *De Romano Pontifice*, Book II, Chapter 29.

78   Francisco Suarez, *De Fide*, Disp. X, Sec. VI, N. 16.

79   Juan de Torquemada, *Summa de ecclesia*, Venice, M. Tranmezium, 1561, Book 2, Chapter 49, p. 163B, emphasis added.

actions endanger the faith of Catholics or otherwise harm the common
good of the Church. Here is St. Thomas' answer to the question,
"Whether a man is *bound* to correct his prelate":

> "It must be observed, however, that if the faith were
> endangered, a subject *ought to rebuke his prelate* even
> publicly. Hence Paul, who was Peter's subject, rebuked him
> in public, on account of the imminent danger of scandal
> concerning faith...."[80]

(St. Peter had unwittingly given scandal to the Gentile converts
in Antioch by making an appearance of continuing to follow some
of the Mosaic dietary laws by refusing to eat with the baptized,
uncircumcised Gentiles.[81]) This teaching of St. Paul and the Catholic
Church is because the Mosaic ceremonial law was — after the
Crucifixion — now forbidden to be practiced by Christians. St.
Thomas notes that resistance to teaching or practices against the Faith
by anyone — even the Pope — is neither unlawful nor presumptuous,
but is both a *duty* and an *act of charity*.

We could continue multiplying examples of such teachings by
Church Doctors and Saints, but I hope that the point is made. There
are no personality cults in the Catholic Church. We have no license
to turn off our minds and follow an authority figure to Heaven. For
Heaven's sake, remember Our Lord's warning (repeated many times
by Sister Lucy) that when the blind follow the blind, they both fall
into the pit! (And Sister Lucy, as if it were the essence of the Third
Secret, spoke of the diabolical disorientation of high churchmen in
our time. We need to be careful not to follow those who knowingly
follow the devil or who even unwittingly do the devil's bidding
because they are themselves so confused.)

As Catholics, we sometimes have not only the right but even
the *duty* to voice our loyal obedience to God and our opposition to
the errors of doctrine or practice advanced by our lawful superiors
who are going beyond their legitimate authority. When the Pope
speaks not in line with the Ordinary and Universal Magisterium,
we have to use our prudence in receiving his teaching. There is

---

80   St. Thomas Aquinas, *Summa Theologica*, II-II, Q. 33, A. 4, ad. 2.
81   *Cf.* Galatians 2:11-14.

no temerity on our part in refusing an assent to any such teaching which is a novelty. And when it is manifestly at odds with prior Church teaching, we must not ever accept this erroneous and/or heretical teaching.

Ambiguous Documents

The primary purpose of an Ecumenical Council is to *clarify* the Catholic Faith, distinguishing the Church's teachings from the errors of the day. Thus the documents of a Church Council must be written in such a way that everyone understands them *in the same sense*. If the documents are unclear, they will only be a source of greater confusion.

John XXIII's decision that the Second Vatican Council would refrain from issuing any dogmatic definitions was, in effect, an open door to carelessness in the language of the Council documents. Not only could these documents be *drafted* in imprecise terms, but they could also be easily *forced through* the voting process, as mere pastoral declarations not requiring careful scrutiny. Bishop Thomas Morris recalls his "relief" at learning of the Council's non-infallible theological note, and he admits that this casual attitude led him to give approval to documents which he knew had been sloppily worded:

> "I was relieved when we were told that this Council was not aiming at defining or giving final statements on doctrine, because a statement of doctrine has to be very carefully formulated, and I ... regarded the Council documents as tentative and likely to be reformed."[82]

Bishop Rudolf Graber was another to comment on the connection between the Council's "pastoral orientation" and what he called the "opalescent ambivalence" of its documents.[83]

---

82 "A Bishop's Candid Memories of Vatican II," January 22, 1997, http://www.catholicculture.org/news/features/indexcfm?recnum=4091&repos=4&subrepos=1&searchid=1265687

83 "Since the Council was aiming primarily at a pastoral orientation and hence refrained from making dogmatically binding statements or disassociating itself, as previous Church assemblies have done, from errors and false doctrines by means of clear anathemas, many questions took on an opalescent ambivalence which provided a certain amount of justification for those who speak of the spirit of the Council." (Rudolf Graber, *Athanasius and the Church of Our Times*, Van Duren, 1974, p. 66)

Rome has been in damage-control mode since the first moment (literally) of promulgating Vatican II's documents. After the constitution *Lumen Gentium* had already been approved by the Council, a group of bishops brought to the Pope's attention a theological error in the document regarding apostolic collegiality. The document wrongly suggests that the supreme authority of the Church resides not in the Pope, but in the apostolic college, which the Pope represents as its head. Father Ralph Wiltgen tells us that, "Pope Paul, realizing finally that he had been deceived, broke down and wept."[84]

The Pope immediately required the Council's theological commission to affix an **introductory** note (the famous "*Nota praevia*") to *Lumen Gentium*, clarifying and correcting the constitution's teaching on collegiality. But against the Pope's wishes, it was relegated to an appendix. Romano Amerio points out this procedure was an utter anomaly "in the whole history of the Church's councils," and that it defies explanation how "the council should issue a doctrinal document so imperfect as to require an explanatory note at the very moment of its promulgation."[85]

Lumen Gentium contains another notorious example of imprecise language open to interpretations flatly opposed to Catholic teaching. In Paragraph 8, we are told that the Church established by Christ in this world *subsists in* the Catholic Church.[86] The question is thus raised: Is the Roman Catholic Church *exclusively identified* here as the true Church of Christ, or is that true Church something larger which merely *includes* the Catholic Church? And if the Catholic Church *IS* the one true Church of Christ, outside of which no one at all is saved, why not say so?!

Of course, we know from the constant teaching of the Catholic Church down through the ages, from the very beginning of the Church to Pope Pius XII, that the Catholic Church **is** the one true

---

84   Father Ralph Wiltgen, *The Rhine Flows into the Tiber*, Hawthorn Books, 1967, p. 232.

85   Romano Amerio, *Iota Unum*, p. 91.

86   "This Church constituted and organized in the world as a society, subsists in the Catholic Church, which is governed by the successor of Peter and by the Bishops in communion with him...." (*Lumen gentium*, paragraph 8.) See also Walter M. Abbott, S.J., ed., *Documents of Vatican II* (New York: The America Press, 1966), page 23.

Church of Jesus Christ. All other churches are false churches! But who today gives you such a clear answer in the Vatican?

Here we begin to sense a sinister purpose in these ambiguous expressions. Can we really explain such a statement as just careless language? There is little doubt that the authors of the Council documents intended to exploit the ambiguity in those documents. The time would come when more precise but openly heretical statements would follow, claiming to have the endorsement of those loosely phrased Council documents.

This particular statement in *Lumen Gentium*, for instance, was an essential steppingstone toward the bolder assertions that have been the staple of certain so-called leading churchmen who claim to be giving "Catholic" teaching for the past fifty years. Here is an example of how the Council's ambiguous language is now generally understood and explained:

> "The Church of Jesus Christ is not exclusively identical with the Roman Catholic Church [Editor's note: this is heresy]. It does indeed subsist in Roman Catholicism, but it is also present in varying modes and degrees in other Christian communities to the extent that they too are faithful to what God initiated in Jesus and are obedient to the inspirations of Christ's Spirit. As a result of their common sharing in the reality of the one Church, the several Christian communities already have with one another a real but imperfect communion."[87]

May God help us. *This truly is heresy!*

Fifty years after the Council, in 2007, the Congregation for the Doctrine of the Faith publicly recognized the need of a special document for the purpose of "clarifying the authentic meaning of some ecclesiological expressions" used by the Council, which the Congregation admits "are open to misunderstanding."[88] Precisely.

---

87   Cardinal Avery Dulles, S.J., cited in *Toward Vatican III: The Work That Needs to Be Done*, ed. David Tracy and Hans Küng, Seabury Press, 1978, p. 91. This teaching of Dulles is heresy.

88   Congregation for the Doctrine of the Faith, "Responses to Some Questions Regarding Certain Aspects of the Doctrine on the Church," June 29, 2007, 3rd paragraph of the Introduction;   http://www.vatican.va/roman_curia/congregations/cfaith/documents/rc_con_cfaith_doc_20070629_responsa-quaestiones_en.html

The documents were written in such a way as to be *open to misunderstanding*. As such, they lack the most important quality needed in an exposition of doctrine: *clarity*.

An "Evil" Council

Many Catholics might find it hard to believe that a Church council could be *evil*. If they don't know very much Church history, and are unaware of what incredibly rough times the Church has been through, they might say that an "evil council" is a contradiction in terms. But it isn't. There have been at least two such councils before our time — one an Ecumenical Council and one a Synod.

Let's first define what *evil* means (using St. Augustine[89] and St. Thomas Aquinas[90] as our guides), and then examine how the word could apply to a Church council.

The ancient Manichaean heretics thought of evil as one of the principles of the universe, having a necessary existence — no less necessary than God's existence. The same dualistic nonsense is the basis of the "Star Wars" story, which (blasphemously) gives far too much credit to the "dark side."

Actually, in itself, evil is … nothing. It's like a hole in a bucket. Evil exists only *in relation to the good*, as the *lack of a good* that ought to be there. Goodness, Truth, and Beauty, these are the realities of both time and eternity. Where we find them lacking in some way in people, places, or things that we know should be there then we call that *privation* of the good, *evil*.

This is easy to grasp in the sense of *physical* evils. If we see a man with only one leg, we call him lame. When a man loses his sight or hearing, we call him blind or deaf. But we don't say these things about stones, even though they can't walk, or see, or hear. What's the difference? It is part of our nature as men to be able to do these things. The lack of natural qualities in particular men, is an evil. If a man does not see — because he has no eyes — we call him blind, because he suffers the physical evil of blindness. A stone or rock does not see, but we do not call it blind — we call it sightless.

Common experience and grammatical expression expresses what

89   St. Augustine, *De Diversis Quaestionibus* 83, Q. 21.

90   St. Thomas Aquinas, *Summa Theologica*, I, Q. 49.

we know instinctively regarding evil. We never say, "Look at that blind stone". We instinctively know that a stone does not see. We are not astonished by the fact that this particular stone or rock does not see. If we need to describe the phenomenon, we use the precise language that that rock is sightless. On the other hand, when we are talking to a friend about a second friend, "You do not understand that our friend is blind — he cannot see." We instinctively know that a man by his very nature is capable of sight. But in the case of Mr. X, our friend, he is an exception because he is blind. Language and culture recognize universally that a physical evil such as blindness or deafness is a lack of what normally should be there. It has been left to the great intellect of St. Thomas and St. Augustine to point out to us that "evil" — whether physical or moral — is a deprivation, a lack of what by nature should be there. This insight — although simple — is a great discovery and a great articulation.[91]

The same is true about *moral* evil. It's no crime for a deer to run from every danger, because God gave it speed as its best defense. But we call a man a coward if he thinks only of escaping confrontations, regardless of his duties. He lacks the courage that we expect to find in a virtuous man (in a *good* man). Our Creator made us good, and part of our purpose as His creatures is that we *be* good. Vice and sin are basically a lack of the good order that ought to be in our actions.

Getting back to the idea of an evil council: All human endeavors have consequences, whether good or evil, and — as Our Lord tells us — "By their fruits you shall know them. … A good tree cannot bring forth evil fruit."[92] If the fruits are evil, so is the tree.

If a lawyer, drawing up a contract between two people, uses ambiguous language (or, worse, *equivocal* language, which is not just unclear, but is *intended* to be interpreted in conflicting ways), he defeats the purpose of the contract. That document was supposed to make clear to the parties precisely what they are agreeing to do for each other. Now instead, it will be a source of confusion and an occasion of disagreements between them. That would be an evil document — because the document lacks a quality that must be there. In this example the contract lacks clarity.

---

91   The Manicheans, for centuries, have misunderstood this concept.

92   Matthew 7:16, 18.

The same is true for the documents of a Church council. What is the purpose of a council? It is to *clarify* the Catholic Faith — to preserve and foster the *unity of belief* and living within the Church, so that (as St. Paul says), "with one mind, and with one mouth, [we] may glorify God."[93] What quality must a council's documents have in order to fulfill this purpose? *Clarity.*

If a council's documents lack clarity, and if its teachings therefore cause confusion and division among the faithful, then by the simple definition of the word, that is an *evil* council. The lack of clarity in the documents is itself an evil, and the documents themselves are evil insofar as they present an obstacle to our unity of belief and unity of common life within the Church according to the Church's rule of Faith. The council that produced these evil documents is the bad tree that brought forth the evil fruit — i.e. evil documents.

There is no irreverence in saying this, unless Pope St. Gregory the Great can be accused of irreverence toward the Second Council of Constantinople! That Council, in 553 A.D., produced ambiguous documents that confused Catholics instead of clarifying the Faith for them. It was still causing problems forty years later, until finally Saint Gregory told the bishops to just ignore those council documents. He said in effect, "Carry on with the Faith according to its prior, clear expressions, and pretend that the Council of 553 never happened."

The Synod of Pistoia was another evil council. In 1786, the Bishop of Pistoia, Italy, convoked a Synod in his diocese with a view toward changing the Mass into vernacular languages, and asserting the authority of bishops against that of the Pope. Pope Pius VI condemned the decrees of the Synod of Pistoia in a bull of 1794, called *Auctorem Fidei*, for confusing teachings which had been clear before the Synod.

For the same reason, it is no exaggeration to say that the fruits of Vatican II have been evil, and that its documents are evil. It is not by coincidence that so much confusion followed the Council. The *ambiguity* of the documents *gave rise* to the confusion in the Church.

To this day, theologians are still debating and trying to explain what the Council "really" taught. Even these defenders of the Council are implicitly admitting that the documents require

---

93   Romans 15:6.

clarification[94] — and therefore that the documents were evil, that the Council itself was evil, and that its fruits have been evil. Most importantly, there is good reason to believe that *Our Lady of Fatima Herself* used these very words, "*an evil council*" (referring to the Second Vatican Council),[95] in the Third Secret — a warning which, according to Her *express order*,[96] was to be published in 1960![97]

Pope Paul VI himself lamented these bitter fruits of the Council, which had become immediately apparent, and plagued the entirety of his pontificate:

1968: "The Church finds Herself in an hour of anxiety, a disturbed period of self-criticism, or what would even better be called *self-destruction*. It is an interior upheaval, acute

94 "[A]fter the Second Vatican Council something happened that had never happened in the aftermath of any council in history, namely that two (or more) contrary hermeneutics [theories of interpretation] found themselves in conflict and, to use the words of the Pope himself, 'quarreled' with each other. ... The existence of a plurality of hermeneutics ... is evidence of a certain ambiguity or ambivalence of the documents. If one must resort to a hermeneutic criterion external to the document in order to interpret the document itself, it is obvious, in fact, that the document is not sufficiently clear in itself." (Roberto de Mattei, *The Second Vatican Council: An Unwritten Story*, page x.)

95 See Father Paul Kramer, "The Secret Warned Against Vatican Council II and the New Mass", *The Fatima Crusader*, Issue 92, May 2009, pp.7ff.

96 On May 31, 2007, Cardinal Bertone made a live remote-feed appearance on the popular Italian television program, *Porta a Porta* ("Door to Door"), in an attempt to defend his crumbling Party Line claims about the Third Secret. Forced by Italian journalist Antonio Socci to retreat from his prior claims that there was only *one envelope* associated with the Third Secret, and that Sister Lucy had herself *invented* the 1960 time-frame, the Cardinal held up before the camera *two envelopes*, each bearing this inscription in Sister Lucy's handwriting: "*By express order of Our Lady, this envelope can only be opened in 1960 by the Cardinal Patriarch of Lisbon or the Bishop of Leiria.*" (*Cf.* Christopher Ferrara, *The Secret Still Hidden*, Pound Ridge, New York, Good Counsel Publications, 2008, pp. 126-127.)

97 Cardinal Alfredo Ottaviani, Pro-Prefect of the Holy Office, interviewed Sister Lucy about the Third Secret of Fatima on May 17, 1955, and he questioned her specifically about the significance of the year 1960. He made parts of that interview known when he spoke at a February 11, 1967 meeting at the Pontifical Marian Academy in Rome, recalling: "The message was not to be opened before 1960. I asked Sister Lucy, 'Why this date?' She answered, '*Because then it will seem clearer.*'" (Cited in Frère Michel, *The Whole Truth About Fatima*, Vol. III, pp. 474 and 721ff.)
        What can this mean, except that the prophecies of the Third Secret would *begin to be realized* at that time? (It was on January 29, 1959 that John XXIII announced his decision to convoke the Second Vatican Council. The Council was convened in 1962.) Clearly, *we are living through the period that Our Lady spoke of in the Third Secret!*

and complicated, which nobody expected after the Council. It is almost as if the Church were attacking itself. We looked forward to a flowering, a serene expansion of conceptions which matured in the great sessions of the Council. But one must notice above all the sorrowful aspect. It is as if the Church were destroying Herself."[98]

1972: "We have the impression that through some cracks in the wall *the smoke of Satan has entered the temple of God*: it is doubt, uncertainty, questioning, dissatisfaction, confrontation. ... We thought that after the Council a day of sunshine would have dawned for the history of the Church. What dawned, instead, was a day of clouds and storms, of darkness, of searching and uncertainties."[99]

Nothing more needs to be said. The very Pope who presided over the Second Vatican Council gave the definitive diagnosis of the confusion, the diabolical disorientation, that has afflicted the Church almost from the moment the Council, with all its unprecedented ambiguities, came to a close.

98   Address to the Lombard Seminary at Rome, December 7, 1968, 7th paragraph, emphasis added;http://www.va/holy_father/paul_vi/speeches/1968/december/documents/hf_p-vi_spe_19681207_seminario-lombardo_it.html

99   Sermon during the Mass for Saints Peter and Paul in St. Peter's Basilica, on the occasion of the ninth anniversary of his coronation, June 29, 1972, 13th paragraph, emphasis added; http://www.vatican.va/holy_father/paul_vi/homilies/1972/documents/hf_p-vi_hom_19720629_it.html

Chapter 3

Lessons from Church History – Even Popes, Councils and Bishops Can Err

The preceding chapters have made it clear that the failure to preserve belief in Catholic dogma, predicted in the Third Secret of Fatima and taking place before our eyes today, must involve a failure of much of the upper hierarchy: bishops, Cardinals, and to a certain extent even the Popes themselves. But how is it possible for the Church's leadership to err in this way? Did Our Lord not promise that the gates of hell would not prevail against His Church? Yes, He certainly did, but that promise does not preclude errors on the part of the Church's leadership that harm the Church even if Her official teaching remains intact. While the gates of hell will not *prevail* against the Church in the sense that the Church would ever formally defect from the Truth and officially teach error, which is impossible, this does not mean that individual churchmen — even the vast majority of them, as during the time of the Arian heresy — can never fail in their defense of the Faith. They can and they have.

For forty days after His Resurrection, Our Lord conversed with the Apostles, "appearing to them, and speaking of the kingdom of God."[100] At last, with His final commission to them just before His Ascension, and with the Descent of the Holy Ghost upon them nine days later, they received such an abundant infusion of grace that for the rest of their lives, they would be able to *avoid ever committing a mortal sin*, and to avoid even ever committing a fully deliberate venial sin.

Each of the Apostles was also given the extraordinary prerogative of personal *infallibility* in matters of faith and morals, whenever they

---

100   Acts 1:3.

taught and imposed a doctrine as an obligatory teaching of the Faith.

These privileges were *personal* graces given to each of the Apostles.

The bishops of the Catholic Church are the true successors of the Apostles, but they (as a whole) have not inherited the personal guarantees of holiness and infallibility that were given to the Apostles. Only the Bishop of Rome, who is St. Peter's successor as Pope, retains the charism of infallibility preserving him from error, and this charism is engaged only *when he is defining* a dogma of Faith or morals. At all other times, the Pope bears the same liability to human weakness and error as do all the other bishops of the world.

The history of the Church has fully borne this truth out.[101] Truly, as all Catholics should know, the Pope can make mistakes — such as personal sins — through *imprudence* and weakness. The Pope can be wrong about what policies will best enable the Church to serve Our Lord. And yes, the Pope can also be mistaken in his beliefs and even in his public teaching, even *about Faith and morals*, when his infallibility is not engaged.

"To Err Is Human..."

Every human being is prone to making mistakes in judgment. We look for the best course to take in particular situations, but in spite of our best efforts, we sometimes get it wrong, or succumb to external pressures. This is true even of a Pope.

Let's look at five examples in the history of the Church, in which a Pope has had the misfortune of seriously blundering. In each of these cases, the consequent harm to the Church would have been even greater if there had not been clearer-thinking, courageous subordinates on hand who understood their duty to resist the Pope's error.

1) Saint Peter, our first and greatest Pope, once acted in such a way that he gave the impression to many who observed him that a condemned error was the Church's true doctrine. He himself understood and believed the true doctrine, of course, and he was

---

101   This present chapter will explore in detail several historical instances of this kind.

acting with the best intentions, trying to maintain peace in the Church, but nevertheless he was causing people to waver in their belief in a defined dogma of Faith.

Here's what happened. In the very earliest days of the Church, the Jewish converts continued to observe some of the customs that had been prescribed by the Mosaic Law — "to bury the synagogue with honor," as it were, as Bishop Richard Challoner says.[102] At the same time, there was a significant number of Pharisees among the first Jewish converts to Christianity, some of whom were insisting that the Gentile converts must also adopt these practices that the Jews had always been required to observe — namely, circumcision and certain dietary laws. The question quickly produced a bitter controversy in the infant Church:

> "That the Church was open to the Gentiles no less than to the Jews had very early been made clear in a vision[103] to St. Peter. ... But were such Gentiles, converted now to the Church, to live as Jews? The Jewish element in the Church continued to practice all the observances of the Mosaic piety. Must the Gentile convert do as much? Did he come to Christ through Judaism or directly? The question was a practical one. It involved such things as circumcision, an elaborate code of dietary regulations, a whole way of life. But it did not end there. The controversy was, at bottom, a controversy as to the relation of the Church to the old religion of the Jews. ... The discussion between the two types of Christian was a discussion as to whether ... a Christian could be saved through the Church alone — ... whether the Church was self-sufficient or, though a better kind of Judaism, still no more than a Jewish sect and, as

---

102 In his gloss on Acts 21:24 in the Douay-Rheims Bible.

103 "I saw in an ecstasy of mind a vision, a certain vessel descending, as it were a great sheet let down from heaven by four corners, and it came even unto me. Into which looking, I considered, and saw four-footed creatures of the earth, and beasts, and creeping things, and fowls of the air: And I heard also a voice saying to me: Arise, Peter; kill and eat. And I said: Not so, Lord; for nothing common or unclean hath ever entered into my mouth. And the voice answered again from heaven: What God hath made clean, do not thou call common. And this was done three times: and all were taken up again into heaven." (Acts 11:5-10)

such, tied to the Law."[104]

The Apostles and other bishops of the Church gathered to decide the question. We read in the Acts of the Apostles how Peter himself settled the matter at the Church's first council, the Council of Jerusalem, in 49 A.D.:

> "[T]here arose some of the sect of the Pharisees that believed, saying: They must be circumcised, and be commanded to observe the law of Moses. ... [And] coming down from Judea, [they] taught the brethren: That *except you be circumcised after the manner of Moses, you cannot be saved.* ... And the apostles and ancients assembled to consider of this matter. And when there had been much disputing, Peter, rising up, said to them: Men, brethren, you know, that ... God, who knoweth the hearts, ... put no difference between us and them, purifying their hearts by faith. Now therefore, why tempt you God to put a yoke upon the necks of the disciples, which neither our fathers nor we have been able to bear? ... Then it pleased the apostles and ancients, ... to send to Antioch, ... writing by their hands: ... Forasmuch as we have heard, that some going out from us have troubled you with words, *subverting your souls*; to whom we gave no commandment: ... It hath seemed good to the Holy Ghost and to us, to lay no further burden upon you than these necessary things: That you abstain from things sacrificed to idols, and from blood, and from things strangled, and from fornication; from which things keeping yourselves, you shall do well. ... Which when they had read, they rejoiced for the consolation. ... And Paul and Barnabas continued at Antioch, teaching and preaching, with many others, the word of the Lord."[105]

So the Council of Jerusalem had taught infallibly that the Catholic faithful were not bound by the Mosaic ceremonial law, including the prohibition against eating with the uncircumcised.

---

104   Rev. Philip Hughes, *A History of the Church to the Eve of the Reformation*, Vol. I, *Beginnings to Byzantine Catholicism*, Veritas Splendor Publications, 2012, p. 66 (Chapter 2, Section 2).

105   Acts 15:1-35, emphasis added.

But the "circumcision" party, as Saint Paul calls them,[106] didn't just go away. In spite of the Council's definition, these "Judaizers" (the "false brethren" to whom Saint Paul refers in his letters to the Corinthians[107] and to the Galatians[108]) naturally still had very strong sensitivities against the foods and practices which they had always viewed as defiling. Even if the old practices were no longer legally required, it seemed to the Judaizers that the observance of the Mosaic customs was the mark of a more perfect Christian. In their eyes, the Gentile converts were merely second-class members of the Church.

Soon after the Council, Peter made a visit to the Christian community at Antioch, where Paul and Barnabas resided, and at first he made no scruple about eating with the uncircumcised Gentile converts. As Pope, he had defined their liberty as Christians to remain uncircumcised, and he knew that they were in no sense "unclean." But then it happened that some of these Judaizers also came to Antioch from Jerusalem (where the Apostle St. James the Less was the bishop).

Peter knew that he had *no obligation* to eat with the Gentile converts, and he knew that his doing so would offend the Judaizers. It must have seemed to Peter that the best course would be to make allowances for the sensitivities of the former Pharisees, and to avoid a needless confrontation with them. So as soon as these former Pharisees arrived, Peter changed his habit and began to eat only with other former Jews.

Of course, this was noticed by everyone, and the unspoken message (though not intended) was: "The Gentile converts are low-class Christians. They can't be sure of their salvation unless they are circumcised and observe the old ceremonial laws." Thus, what Peter's example really amounted to was a *dissimulation* — giving a false impression — in favor of the error which he had already formally condemned.

By shunning the Gentile converts, Saint Peter was leading many

106 *Cf.* Galatians 2:12; Colossians 4:11; Titus 1:10.

107 "...in perils from false brethren." (2 Corinthians 11:26)

108 "But because of false brethren unawares brought in, who came in privately to spy our liberty, which we have in Christ Jesus, that they might bring us into servitude." (Galatians 2:4) Saint Paul explains the Church's teaching on this question at length in his letters to the Galatians and to the Romans.

Christians at Antioch toward a heretical belief, as if the infallible teaching of the Council of Jerusalem had been wrong. So powerful was his example, in fact, that a great many of the Jewish converts were led into the same shameful practice of refusing to eat with the Gentile converts. Saint Paul tells us that even Saint Barnabas — who had been set aside with Saint Paul at the command[109] of the Holy Ghost to preach to the Gentiles, and who himself had worked miracles demonstrating the election of the Gentiles and the abrogation of the Old Law — had lost his sense of the Church's true doctrine.

Saint Peter did not personally embrace this error, and he didn't realize that his condescension to the Judaizers was giving a heretical impression to the faithful, but that was the fact, nevertheless. Finally Saint Paul corrected Saint Peter — *in public*, before all those people who had been misled by Peter's bad example. Saint Paul stood alone and said, basically, "Your Holiness, you're wrong and you can't do this":

> "But when Cephas was come to Antioch, I withstood him to the face, because he was to be blamed. For before that some came from James, he did eat with the Gentiles: but when they were come, he withdrew and separated himself, fearing them who were of the circumcision. And to his dissimulation the rest of the Jews consented, so that Barnabas also was led by them into that dissimulation. But when I saw that they walked not uprightly unto the truth of the gospel, I said to Cephas before them all: If thou, being a Jew, livest after the manner of the Gentiles, and not as the Jews do, how dost thou compel the Gentiles to live as do the Jews?"[110]

This, by the way, was a marvelous example of *true loyalty* to Saint Peter and to the papacy. All those who had gone along with Peter in "respectful silence", or whatever you want to call it, had not done any service either to him or to the Church (to say the least)! Their cooperation had served only to obscure the true Faith and to jeopardize the salvation of many souls.

To Saint Peter's credit, he quickly realized his error, and he

---

109   *Cf.* Acts 13:2.

110   Galatians 2:11-14.

humbly acknowledged the truth of Saint Paul's correction.

Sadly, this whole incident remains a stumbling-block for many non-Catholics to this day, who deny the authority of the Pope and who misunderstand Saint Paul's resistance. I remember how, even as a seminarian, I was asking myself why God had allowed Saint Peter to make such a mistake, and why He had perpetuated the scandal by inspiring Saint Paul to include an account of the event in his letter to the Galatians. At first glance, this passage seems to make it difficult to defend the Catholic teaching about papal supremacy and authority.

I realize now that God allowed this incident to happen *for our instruction*. It's an important lesson for every generation of the faithful, from that day until the end of time. We need to have clear ideas about the purpose and limits of the Pope's authority, and to understand that the papacy is not meant to be the basis of a personality cult. The Church's hierarchy does not operate by means of slavish and unreflective submission to one's superiors. Blind "obedience" can never justify us in disregarding a defined dogma of the Faith.

2) The Second Council of Constantinople (553 A.D.). Constantinople II, the Church's fifth ecumenical council, offers a strange parallel to the confusion caused by Vatican II. Before Vatican II, the Second Council of Constantinople was called "the strangest of all the general councils."[111] It became embroiled in a misguided attempt to placate exponents of the Monophysite heresy (denying the human nature of Christ) by condemning the controversial writings of three authors that the Monophysite heretics despised, even though those three authors died reconciled with the Church. This misguided effort to "give satisfaction to the Monophysites"[112] in a "tricky attempt to conciliate the Monophysites"[113] failed miserably, and the Church suffered serious damage as a result. "[T]he immediate effect was to produce temporary schisms in the West; and *the successive*

---

111 Philip Hughes, *A History of the Church*, Vol. I: *The Church and the World in Which the Church Was Founded* (1934: London: Sheed and Ward, republished 1979), p. 282; cited in Ferrara and Woods, *The Great Façade* (Remnant Press: 2002), p. 326.

112 Charles Joseph Hefele, *A History of the Councils of the Church*, Vol. IV, trans. William R. Clark (Edinburgh: T&T Clark, 1895), p. 352; cited in Ferrara and Woods, *The Great Façade,* p. 328.

113 Hughes, *A History of the Church*, Vol. I, p. 280; cited in Ferrara and Woods, p. 328.

contradictory utterances of [Pope] Vigilius did not enhance the authority of the Roman see."[114]

This council was such an embarrassment to the Church that no less than Pope Saint Gregory the Great recommended to the Emperor Constantine that he quell certain disturbances the Council had caused "by not mentioning Constantinople II at all." Note this well: one of the greatest Popes in Church history counseled "remaining silent about the fifth ecumenical council of the Catholic Church."[115]

This shows us that even an ecumenical council can make a serious mistake when it departs from what the Church has always taught and tries to placate heretics, even if the council does not formally teach heresy. The comparison with the problems caused by Vatican II is very informative.

3) Pope Honorius I. About 550 years after Saint Peter's time, Pope Honorius I was ruling the Church, during the years 625 to 638. Like Saint Peter, Honorius struggled against heresies springing up within the Church, and also like Saint Peter, he found it difficult to balance his desire to preserve the equanimity of the faithful with his duty to root out errors against the Faith.

Honorius' downfall was that in the end, he thought it best to remain silent in the face of errors, when what was actually needed was the authoritative voice of the Magisterium. Unfortunately for Honorius, he lacked Saint Peter's sense to recognize the better course when it was pointed out to him. Pope Honorius is chiefly remembered today as having been an aider and abettor of heresy, and as being roundly condemned for his negligence by subsequent Popes and Councils.

At the heart of the Mystery of our Redemption is the fact that Jesus Christ is not only true God, but also true Man. The Second Person of the Blessed Trinity, "when the fullness of time had come,"[116] took to Himself a complete human nature, and was thus able — as a true member of the human race — to offer satisfaction to God for the

---

114 Henry Chadwick, *The Early Church* (New York: Penguin, 1993), p. 210; cited in Ferrara and Woods, p. 329.

115 Ferrara and Woods, op. cit., p. 330.

116 Galatians 4:4.

sin of Adam. Being true Man, He could *atone* for the sins of men, and being true God, His acts of Atonement were infinitely meritorious, able to superabundantly repair the offenses of all men.

The early centuries of the Church saw various heresies about Our Lord. In the 4th Century, the followers of Arius[117] denied that Jesus Christ was true God equal to God the Father and consubstantial with God the Father. Then in the 5th Century, the followers of Nestorius,[118] on another extreme, exaggerated Our Lord's human nature to the extent that it was regarded as a separate person in itself. Nestorius blasphemously claimed that Our Lady was the mother only of Our Lord's human nature, and not of His Divine Person, thus denying Her prerogative as the true Mother of God. But, of course, Jesus Christ is only one Person, and He (though God) was born of the Virgin Mary, His Mother.

Another heresy regarding the Incarnation arose in the 7th Century. While Nestorius' teachings about Our Lord's distinct natures would practically separate Christ into two different Persons (one human and the other divine), the doctrine of the "Monothelites" was to assert that Christ's two natures were so completely joined that the one Person, Jesus Christ, had only a single principle of activity, or *will*. The undivided Word, they said, must have an undivided activity, and therefore a single *theandric* or "Divino-human" will.

The true Catholic doctrine is that Jesus Christ's two natures (His eternal divine nature and His created human nature) are *hypostatically* united in His one single Person, and that His human nature remains complete, both in body *and soul*. Now, a soul has the faculties of both intellect and *will*, and this *will* is an essential property of human nature. Thus it is the Catholic teaching that Our Lord, though only one Person, has two distinct wills. Therefore, Our Lord's actions are distinguished according to their source as being either *divine activities* or *human activities*. We also know, of course, that Our Lord's human will was always completely obedient to the Divine Will, as we see from His words in the Garden of Olives, "Not *My*

---

117 A priest in Alexandria, Egypt. He died A.D. 336. Arianism was condemned at the First Council of Nicea in 325 A.D.

118 The Patriarch of Constantinople from 428-431. Nestorianism was condemned at the Council of Ephesus in 431 A.D.

will but *Thine* be done."[119]

The sad situation in Honorius' time was that the Church in Syria and Egypt was deeply infected with a heresy regarding the Hypostatic Union. Worse, in the beginning of that heresy, that heresy was so misunderstood by Western Church leaders (because of language issues) that almost all efforts to combat the errors were wasted on non-issues.

The Catholic dogma of the union of the divine and human natures in the one Person of Christ, had been solemnly defined by Pope Saint Leo the Great in the year 449,[120] and reiterated by the Council of Chalcedon in 451.[121] In these definitions affirming Our Lord's two natures, the word *nature* was used in the sense of an essence without a subject. But the Eastern Catholics read the word in the sense in which St. Cyril had insisted on "one nature" in Christ, meaning a *subsistent nature*, including its subject, and thus the equivalent of our term *hypostasis*. So the Eastern bishops were accusing the Western Church of teaching that there are *two Persons* in Christ, while the Western bishops supposed the Eastern leaders to hold that the *human nature* of Christ was so swallowed up by His divine nature as to *no longer exist*.

This source of the confusion only became apparent after many years. In Honorius' day, Western apologists were wasting their energies trying to prove the fact of a true human nature in Christ against these supposedly *Monophysite* (or "one-nature") heretics, as they called them, whereas the real error of the Eastern heresy was in diminishing Our Lord's free will, as if His human nature lacked a properly human power of action. So the "Monophysites" actually accepted the teaching of the two natures of Christ, but they denied that He had two effective wills, or that His actions could be divided into two categories, divine and human.

The history of this heresy involves an amazing chain of events, almost a "comedy of errors" if it were not all so deadly serious. Let us here outline briefly the history of events and the main characters involved in the historical unfolding of this heresy.

The **emperor Heraclius** passed through Armenia in the year

---

119   Luke 22:42.

120   *Cf.* Dz. 143-144, D.S. 290-295.

121   *Cf.* Dz. 148, D.S. 300-302.

622, and a certain religious leader named Paul made a speech before him favoring the Monophysite beliefs. Heraclius responded and successfully refuted Paul (or so he thought), describing Our Lord's activities as proceeding from "one operation." (Of course, in saying this, the emperor was unknowingly affirming the Monophysite creed, and not the Catholic Faith.)

A local **bishop** named **Cyrus**[122] was impressed at how deftly the emperor had managed to bring the Monophysite into agreement with the "Catholic" position, but he was also more than a little suspicious of that expression, "one operation." So in about the year 626, Cyrus — all but convinced that the emperor's exposition of the Faith was flatly wrong — wrote to ask the advice of **Sergius**, the **Patriarch of Constantinople**. Cyrus quoted for Sergius the definition of Pope St. Leo that in Our Lord, "*each nature does what is proper to it* with the mutual participation of the other,"[123] as plainly referring to two distinct but inseparable operations.

Sergius admitted that the question was too weighty for him to decide alone, but he sent to Cyrus a copy of a letter that his predecessor Mennas had sent to Pope Vigilius, which the Pope had approved, and which cited several authorities for the teaching that Our Lord acted from one operation and one will. (Sergius did not realize that this supposed letter of Patriarch Mennas was actually a forgery produced by the Monophysites in an attempt to bolster belief in their heresy.)

Sergius was the "top-dog" of the East, being the Patriarch of the most influential Eastern see. So (amazingly) in spite of the definitions of St. Leo the Great and of the Council of Chalcedon, Cyrus thought it best to defer to Sergius. He blandly took Sergius' reply to be a confirmation that the term "one operation" had good authority as an expression of the Catholic teaching on the Incarnation!

Then in the year 630, the emperor chose Cyrus to be the Patriarch of Alexandria, Egypt — a region teeming with Monophysites. Cyrus set about trying to reconcile these people to the true Faith, and he drew up a series of propositions to which the sectarians would have to subscribe in order to be reconciled to the Church. In these propositions, he described Our Lord as "working His divine and His

---

122   Bishop of the ancient town of Phasis, on the eastern coast of the Black Sea.

123   Dz. 144, D.S. 294.

human works by one theandric operation,"[124] imitating Heraclius' expression, and hoping for the same happy results.

To his delight, the majority of heretics in his see were willing to accept the propositions, and great numbers of Monophysites were received back into the Catholic Church. This success of Cyrus' efforts was, of course, noted throughout the East, and Cyrus was making a great name for himself.

It's not difficult now to see why the Monophysites were so easily won over by Cyrus' formulas: They found them perfectly acceptable expressions of their own heresy. Cyrus' propositions *did not* express the Catholic Faith and, moreover, the Monophysites had never held the error which he supposed them to be renouncing!

Here was a pathetic situation, but God sent a saint to point the way back to the truth — Saint Sophronius. Tragically, both the saint and the truth found little welcome. Saint Sophronius stood practically alone in trying to correct the state of affairs, and to little avail.

Our saint was a monk with a great reputation for holiness, living under the direction of a holy hermit near Bethlehem for more than twenty years. In 633, Sophronius went to Egypt to plead — on his knees — before Cyrus to abandon his heretical seventh proposition, but the great Cyrus took no account of him. Saint Sophronius then went to Constantinople and urged Sergius to admonish Cyrus. Sergius was not convinced by Sophronius' arguments that "two operations" was the only acceptable expression of the Catholic teaching, but he agreed to stop using the expression "one operation" on his own part, and even to write to Cyrus suggesting that he also avoid the expression in future discourses. Sergius also rightly saw fit to set the whole matter before the Pope.

As Sergius prepared his now-famous letter of 634 to Pope Honorius, Saint Sophronius made his way back to Palestine, where in the same year he was elected against his will as the Patriarch of Jerusalem. As such, he immediately assembled a synod of all the bishops in his Patriarchate to explain and prove the true Catholic Faith against the single-operation heresy which was (now more than ever) tearing the Eastern world away from the Church.

---

124 Seventh *Capitulum.*

Sergius seems to have been more of a politician at heart than a theologian or shepherd of souls. In his letter to Pope Honorius, he shows little concern for the truth. Instead, his emphasis is on the need for defending an expression that the emperor had used, and for not unsettling the wonderful "conversions" that Cyrus had brought about in Alexandria. His recommendation to Honorius was that the Magisterium should carefully *avoid the issue* of whether there is one operation or two operations in Christ, and let sleeping dogs lie, so to speak.

So the whole matter was placed before the Pope, who was the only person who could effectively remedy the disaster. Tragically, the real disaster was yet to come, and it came through the rulings of Pope Honorius himself.

Pope Honorius answered Sergius' letter without a word of correction regarding Cyrus' propositions. The Pope congratulated Sergius for discontinuing his use of the expression "one operation," but he agreed (incredibly) that it would be well also to avoid any effort to correct the heresy. *"We must be careful not to rekindle ancient quarrels,"* he said, as if to justify this silence. "*As regards defining a dogma of the Church*, while confessing there are two natures united in Christ, *we should not definitively state whether there are one or two operations in the Mediator between God and men.*"[125]

The flock of Jesus Christ, which had been entrusted to the care of Honorius, was literally perishing under his very nose for want of sound doctrine. The power of the keys had been given to him for a reason, to be exercised when the good of the Church required it. Here he was, being in a position as the chief pastor of the Church, to rout a widespread heresy practically at its very inception. But instead, he refused to uphold the true doctrine. Father John Chapman comments:

> "It was now for the pope to pronounce a dogmatic decision and save the situation. He did nothing of the sort. His answer to Sergius did not decide the question, did not authoritatively declare the faith of the Roman Church, did not claim to speak with the voice of Peter; it condemned nothing, it

---

125   Pope Honorius I, "Epistola ad Sergium," *Patrologia Latina* by Jacques-Paul Migne (*MPL*), Vol. 80, Column 475.

defined nothing."[126]

The synod of bishops under Saint Sophronius composed a marvelous letter demonstrating the true Catholic dogma from the teaching of the Fathers, and Saint Sophronius sent this epistle to Pope Honorius and to each of his fellow Eastern Patriarchs. But they cared nothing for it. In fact, Honorius rebuked Sophronius for it, and wrote another letter to Sergius urging him even more strongly that in explanations of the Faith, no mention should be made of either one operation or two operations in Christ. **The Pope was adamantly placing the true dogma of the Church under the same ban as the heresy!**

Saint Sophronius — seeing not only the emperor and the majority of Eastern Patriarchs, but even the Pope himself, conspiring against the truth — rightly took this as an indication that he should devote even more energy to denouncing the heresy, and especially the Pope's role in it. He spoke as loudly and plainly as he possibly could, without any undue respect of persons.

Sophronius lived only a few years beyond the time of Honorius' second letter to Sergius (until 638), but before he died he passed the torch of faithful resistance on to the senior bishop of his patriarchate, Stephen, the Bishop of Doria (Doza). Sophronius took Stephen to Mount Calvary and charged him — by Our Lord Who had been crucified there, and before Whom Stephen would have to give an account on the Last Day, if by his delay he allowed the Faith to be further endangered — to go to Rome, and there to urge and beseech the Church leaders unceasingly until they consent to attend to their duty of examining and condemning the Eastern heresy.

(Bishop Stephen did so, returning to Rome repeatedly throughout ten long years of even greater turmoil in the Church, until he saw the Eastern errors condemned by Pope St. Martin I at the Lateran Council of 649. But as we will see, the damage done by Honorius would even then be far from having run its course.)

With the true Catholic dogma effectively suppressed by Pope Honorius, the Patriarch of Constantinople Sergius and the emperor

---

126 Rev. John Chapman, O.S.B., "Honorius I," *The Catholic Encyclopedia*, Robert Appleton Co., New York, 1910, Vol. VII, p. 453.

Heraclius continued to drive the Eastern world even more firmly into heresy. Sergius began by drafting an exposition of faith (or "*ecthesis*") in response to the synodal letter of Saint Sophronius. This exposition was a complete profession of faith based on the five General Councils which had thus far taken place, but it *included a prohibition against any discussion of whether there are one or two operations in Christ*. It also modified some of the language to which Sophronius had objected, substituting the notion that there is only one *energy* in Christ with the explicit assertion that He has only one *will*.

(Thus what the *Ecthesis* actually taught was no less heretical — and scarcely different — than what had before gone by the names of Monophysitism and Monoenergism. The heresy would simply now be expressed in the more proper term *Monothelitism*, referring to one will.)

Emperor Heraclius immediately seized on the *Ecthesis* as a means of restoring some much-needed unity to the East. (All this internal religious division posed a serious threat to the Eastern realm of the empire just then, particularly in light of the growing external threat of a Mohammedan invasion. Syria had been invaded by Muslims from the Arabian Peninsula, and the threat to Mesopotamia, Armenia, and Egypt was keenly felt.) In the year 638, Heraclius published the *Ecthesis* as an imperial edict throughout all four Eastern metropolitan sees, hoping that both East and West would find its modified teaching acceptable.

The edict purported to represent the Church's official doctrine. By order of Heraclius, all subjects of the empire were to avoid alike both expressions, "one operation" or "two operations," and all were to confess that there was only a single, divine will in Christ.

Thus, at the suggestion of Honorius, the true Faith now stood under interdict throughout the entire Christian world.

Saint Sophronius had died earlier that year, so he never saw the *Ecthesis*, but his successor as Patriarch of Jerusalem approved the edict, as did the other eastern Patriarchs. For Sergius had assembled a great council at Constantinople, which (based on the letter of Honorius) speedily accepted the *Ecthesis* as "truly agreeing with the Apostolic teaching," and established its acceptance throughout the East.

Both Honorius and Sergius also died that same year (in October and December, 638, respectively). Sergius survived the close of his council by only a few days.

Patriarch Sergius, as we said, seems to have been concerned above all with simple expediency. However, he quite possibly would have followed Pope Honorius and Patriarch Sophronius in working to restore orthodoxy to the East, had only Pope Honorius not been so grossly negligent of his duties. With the deaths of these three prelates in 638, that window of opportunity for an "easy fix" was closed. Moreover, Sergius' successor, Pyrrhus, was not just another clerical politician — he was a devoted heretic, and each of the Eastern sees was now dead-set against Western influence.

Pope Honorius' successors, on the other hand, were anxious to restore the true Faith to the East, though thanks to Honorius, the task was now practically impossible. Pope Severinus was elected just three days after Honorius' death, but when his envoys went to Constantinople to have his election confirmed by the emperor, Emperor Heraclius insisted that Severinus first sign the *Ecthesis*. The Pope refused, and Heraclius likewise refused to ratify the election, and even went on to persecute the Pope over this matter for the next year and a half, inciting mobs and nobles against him — even plundering the Lateran palace. But Pope Severinus remained firm, and openly condemned the heretical *Ecthesis*.

Finally Emperor Heraclius, weakening with age and seeing that he himself was doing more to tear the empire in half than his edict could ever do to heal the division, finally gave in and ratified the papal election. Pope Severinus was then formally installed in office in May of 640, just two months before his own death. He was followed by a worthy successor in this battle, Pope John IV, who immediately summoned a synod of the Western bishops to formally condemn the *Ecthesis*.

Heraclius died in February of the following year, 641, prematurely broken down by the weight of the disastrous religious controversy. Shortly before his death, he wrote a letter to Pope John disowning the *Ecthesis*, and blaming Sergius for all the damage it had caused. He might have more truly blamed Honorius.

But in spite of disowning the *Ecthesis* before his death, Heraclius did not officially withdraw it as a legal edict. Pope John, in his brief two years on the papal throne, wrote numerous times to the first two successors of Heraclius, demanding that the edict be withdrawn. But unfortunately, Pope John's denunciations of the edict spoke only of its heretical insistence on confessing a single will in Christ — the Pope fell short of placing the rightful blame on *Honorius* for the original error of *forbidding the profession of Our Lord's two wills*. This error was soon to be the central issue dividing East and West, with continued horrible costs.

In 648, Heraclius' grandson Constans II occupied the imperial throne, and the disastrous religious divisions throughout the empire were one of his chief worries. Now since Rome's objections to the *Ecthesis* had been only about the profession of one will, Constans and the Eastern patriarchs understood the Western ruling to still be that it was prohibited to speak about either one or two operations in Christ (this teaching having come from Pope Honorius himself).

Hoping to restore unity to East and West, Constans complied with the Pope's desire that he withdraw the *Ecthesis*. At the same time, however, he replaced it with a law which he thought would be acceptable to the Pope. This new law, called the Type of Constans, forbade (under severe penalties) all discussion of the disputed doctrine, whether in terms of one or two *operations*, or now also even in terms of one or two *wills*. The Type was simply an even bolder, more explicit enshrinement of the error of Honorius, making the Catholic Faith equally forbidden as heresy!

Church historian Monsignor Philip Hughes[127] correctly traces the entire disaster to the negligence of Honorius:

> "Alas, the real fury of the Monothelite heresy had not even begun. The dogmatic question once raised must be settled. Honorius, failing to see the point raised, had set it aside. Sooner or later there would come a pope who, more understanding, could not follow that precedent. Rome must teach, and definitely. On the other hand the imperial prestige was bound up with the new theory. If Rome condemned it the emperor must either submit or fight. No emperor yet

---

127   1895-1967; Professor of Reformation History at the University of Notre Dame.

had surrendered his patronage of heresy at the bidding of a pope. All the emperors who had once adopted heresy had died ultimately in the heresy of their choice — Constantine and Valens in Arianism, Theodosius II compromised with the Monophysites, Zeno and Anastasius in actual schism. Now it was the turn of the family of Heraclius, and once again, heresy, for forty years, finds in the Christian Emperor its chief and only support, while the traditional faith is proscribed and the faithful persecuted."[128]

The Pope in 649 was Saint Martin I, a true shepherd and no hireling. He had been his predecessor's ambassador to Constantinople, and had been given the difficult task of warning and excommunicating that Patriarch three years before. He knew well both the problem and the opponents whom he faced in this issue of the Eastern heresy.

Martin also knew that Our Lord had established the throne of Saint Peter for a reason, and he was ready to do his job — to clarify the true Faith by speaking *ex cathedra*. Martin convened a Council in the Lateran which condemned both the *Ecthesis* and the Type as heretical for forbidding the teaching of two operations and two wills in Christ. No mention was made of Honorius who was responsible for this heresy, but the Council expressed its presumption of Constans' good will in publishing the Type. Patriarch Sergius and Patriarch Cyrus, on the other hand, were anathematized by name.

Constans was shocked, humiliated, and furious. He had Pope Martin seized and brought before the emperor's court in Constantinople. The Pope endured the most pitiable abuse, insults, and even torture, until these finally culminated in his martyrdom in the Crimea in the year 655. Cruel retaliations were also forthcoming from all quarters of the Eastern heretics against the Western faithful, both laity and priests.

As horrible as things had become, the Church had yet to experience the most bitter fruit of Honorius' failings. As many as 400 Eastern bishops assembled at a Council in Constantinople in the year 662, to condemn Saint Martin for his Lateran Council, as if for treason. Predictably, the impious resolutions of this Eastern Council

---

128 Rev. Philip Hughes, *Op. cit.,* Vol. I, p. 394 (Chapter 10, Section 3).

led quickly to a virtual schism between the East and the West, at the cost of only-God-knows how many souls.

Thanks be to God, this schism was not to last for centuries. It was healed twenty years later at the Church's sixth General Council, held in the years 680 and 681. At this Third Council of Constantinople, the true doctrine of the Church regarding the Incarnate Son of God, as had been defined by Pope Leo the Great and at the Council of Chalcedon, was reaffirmed:

> "And so we proclaim two natural wills in Him, and two natural operations...."[129]

In the Council proceedings, the original figures in the controversy were read and discussed. Sophronius was pronounced to have been the defender of the true Faith; Sergius and Cyrus were condemned as the pioneers of heresy. Pope Honorius, too, at last, got his due:

> "[I]n addition to [Sergius, Cyrus, *et al.*] we decide that Honorius also, who was pope of elder Rome, be with them cast out of the holy Church of God, and be anathematized with them, because we have found by his letter to Sergius that he followed his opinion in all things, and confirmed his wicked dogmas."[130]

The proceedings closed with a series of "final acclamations," in which all those assembled shouted an anathema upon the heretics whom the Council had condemned by name. Honorius was included in this litany:

> "To Honorius, the heretic,[131] anathema!"[132]

---

129   Third Council of Constantinople, Session XVIII, September 16, 681; Dz. 291, D.S. 556.

130   Session XIII, March 28, 681; D.S. 552.

131   It is by no means clear that Honorius himself subscribed to the Monothelite heresy. Nevertheless, any act forbidding the profession of the true Faith is heretical for that reason alone, and it is in this sense that Honorius was here condemned — not as a Monothelite, but rather, as the Council had said, because it was apparent from Honorius' letter to Sergius "that he followed his opinion in all things, and confirmed his wicked dogmas." Father Chapman concedes, "It is clear that no Catholic has the right to defend Pope Honorius. He was a heretic, not in intention, but in fact." (*Op. cit.*, p. 455.)

132   Session XVI.

When the Holy Father, Pope Saint Leo II, confirmed the decrees of the Council, he added his own expression of condemnation of Pope Honorius for not having authoritatively taught the unchanging Faith of the Church when an *ex cathedra* definition was so needed, and for instead approving a ban on both the true and heretical professions:

"We anathematize the inventors of the new error, that is, [Sergius, etc.] and also Honorius, *who did not attempt to sanctify this Apostolic Church with the teaching of Apostolic tradition*, but by a sacrilegious treachery permitted its spotless faith to be sullied."[133]

Later, in a letter to the Spanish bishops, Pope Saint Leo remarked again on Honorius' betrayal of his duties, and the disaster that befell the Church through him:

"With Honorius, who did not, as became the Apostolic authority, extinguish the flame of heretical teaching in its first beginning, but fostered it by his negligence."[134]

Saint Sophronius had rightly stood up to Honorius, whose compromising principle was giving free rein to heresy, and suppressing the true Faith. Immeasurable harm was done to the Church — not only by Pope Honorius, but all those who followed him in his error.

4) Pope Paschal II. Moving forward in history by another 500 years, we come to the reign of Pope Paschal II, whose missteps as head of the Church again threatened to seriously compromise the faithful at large. Again, too, those serving beneath the Pope did not hesitate to stand up to him — this time, successfully preventing a disaster.

When Paschal was elected in the year 1099, he inherited as one of the biggest problems of his pontificate the generations-long battle with the Holy Roman Emperors over the privilege of "lay investiture" — that is, the question of who gets to name the next

---

133   Leo II, "Epistola ad Constantinum IV Imperatorem," *MPL* 96, D.S. 563, emphasis added.

134   Cited in Rev. John Chapman, "Honorius I," *The Catholic Encyclopedia*, Vol. VII, p. 455.

bishops or abbots, etc. when vacancies arise.

The struggle to establish the Church's exclusive right to make ecclesiastical appointments was the work of eight successive Popes, beginning with Nicholas II who instituted[135] the electoral College of Cardinals in the year 1059, declaring that secular authorities would no longer be allowed to appoint new Popes. The Emperor, Henry IV, was only nine years old at that time, so the real confrontations between the Church and the German monarchy over Nicholas' correction of this abuse didn't begin until sixteen years later, in 1075, during the pontificate of Saint Gregory VII (1073-1085).

Lay investiture (a practice by which bishop and abbot approvals were decided by the ruling civil authority) was too common a practice in medieval times, not just in the Kingdom of Germany, but also in France under Philip I and in England under William the Conqueror. The highest offices in the Church were all too often awarded by kings and feudal lords not to those who were best fit for spiritual responsibilities, but to those who promised the greatest advantages to the temporal authority, whether in gifts or in subservience. Those charged with leading and defending the Church were often therefore in reality mere vassals of the crown.

Pope Gregory was determined to bring a complete end to this abuse against the Church by secular powers, and in 1075 he declared[136] that the Pope's power was in no way subject to that of any emperor, and that the Pope alone had the right and authority to install, transfer, or depose bishops.

Henry reacted by trying to depose the Pope (setting up anti-pope Clement III as a rival to Pope Gregory) and even by invading Rome with his army. (It was this invasion that led to the Norman sack of Rome in 1084.) Gregory, having excommunicated Henry (which was an astonishingly bold act at that time), died in exile shortly after the German invasion, but history shows him to have been the real victor over Henry, who had destroyed the basis of his own authority over his princes and people by his rebellion against the Church and against the Pope.

We come, then, to the pontificate of Paschal II, who inherited

---

135   *Cf.* Pope Nicholas II, Bull *"In Nomine Domini,"* April 13, 1059.

136   *Cf.* Lenten Synod of Rome, 1075.

this great struggle of the Church against temporal powers in the year 1099. By this time, the focus of the struggle had shifted entirely to the privilege of appointing bishops and abbots, but the Holy Roman Emperor (now Henry's son, Henry V) remained the primary opponent of the Church's rights.

During his father's reign, the younger Henry had been on friendly terms with Paschal. Nevertheless, within a short time of acquiring the throne as Henry V in 1106, he made it clear that he would follow his father's policy of insisting on making Church appointments himself.

By the year 1108, Henry had already been excommunicated by Pope Paschal, but he was still determined to secure his claim to the throne by a proper coronation by the Pope at St. Peter's Basilica in Rome. So in 1110 he came with his army into Italy to be crowned by the Pope, openly threatening at the same time to settle the question of investitures with his sword.

Paschal (possibly in fear for his life) came to an agreement[137] with the emperor on the terms under which the coronation would take place: Henry would renounce all claims to investitures *in exchange for a return of all the temporal rights, privileges, and estates* acquired from the crown by all the bishops in the German realm of the empire since the time of Charlemagne (800 A.D.).

It is not easy for us to understand the significance of what this surrender of lands and their governance would mean to the Church in those far-off, medieval days:

> "[Paschal promised] to make over to the king the whole vast amount, lands, privileges, temporal jurisdiction. Had it been possible to carry out, the treaty would have revolutionized the social structure of half of Europe. To the king it would have conveyed immediately an immense increase of wealth and power. The Church — bishops, abbots, schools, hospitals, pious foundations, the whole vast movement before which still lay the task of Christianizing the Germans and converting the heathen — would just as suddenly be stripped of all its material equipment and its public status while there still lay upon it the burden of maintaining all the life it had called into being in the course

---
137 *Cf.* Concordat of Sutri, April 1111.

of seven centuries; and it would once more, inevitably, have fallen into the lay lords' power."[138]

In our own industrialized world of the 21st Century, completely under the dominance of big-government and of international banks, we can hardly imagine the small-scale, agriculturally-based economy of the medieval world. But before there was any such thing as corporate farms or urban supermarkets supporting whole populations of dispossessed, highly taxed, urban wage-earners, living only from paycheck to paycheck, the Church and the land were the backbone of a self-supporting, predominantly rural society whose economy was based not on monetary wages and debt, but on true *production*. My dear friend Deirdre Manifold (now deceased) described this small-farm economy in her book, *Fatima and the Great Conspiracy*:

"The Catholic Church included in it a great deal more than the business of teaching religion and of practicing worship and administering the Sacraments. It had a great deal to do with the temporal welfare of the people. It provided, and amply provided, for all the wants of the poor and the distressed. It contained a great body of land, proprietors whose revenues were distributed in various ways amongst the people at large, upon terms always singularly advantageous to the tenant. It was a great and powerful estate, independent both of the aristocracy and the Crown, and naturally siding with the people. But above all things, it was a provider for the poor and a keeper of hospitality, and held society together by ties of religion rather than by the trammels and terrors of the law. ...

"From the sixth to the fifteenth century — 900 years — England enjoyed what is known as the golden age of Christianity. In that Golden Age, life revolved around the Church; that is, the life of the common people revolved around the monastery in particular.

138 Rev. Philip Hughes, *Op. cit.*, Vol. II, *The Fall of Rome to the 13th Century*, p. 312 (Chapter 6, Section 1).

"The monasteries possessed land. This was divided up into ... small farms, and leased to farmers on the most favorable and secure terms. The farmer would contribute [from] each harvest a tithe of what he produced, as rent on the land. If [in a certain year the land] produced little or nothing, he paid little or nothing. If he had a good harvest, he gave the tithe. His tenure was of the most secure kind for he did not deal with a personal landlord who could sell his land or pass it on to an erring heir. The farmer had his lease from the monastery and was not the victim of any individual or of his personal whim."[139]

This "independence from the aristocracy" was guaranteed, both *to the Church* and to the peasantry, by the *Church lands*. To cede those lands to the crown would have reduced the bishoprics and abbeys throughout the Kingdom of Germany not only to beggary, but also to *impotence against the temporal powers*. Henry's demands threatened the same disaster for the Church that befell Pope Pius IX when the last of the Papal States were seized from him by the King of Italy in 1870. Without an internal source of goods and revenue, the Church in Germany would have no hope for sustaining its hierarchy's undivided loyalties and true freedom of action.

So when Paschal signed that compact with Henry in the year 1111 (promising that all of the bishops and abbots of Germany would hand over the Church's lands to Henry), the Pope was really promising nothing less than that he and the bishops would *betray* Our Lord and His Church.

Early in the following year, on the appointed day,[140] Paschal promulgated his formal order to the German bishops to return all of the Church's temporalities to the crown. The bishops, however, *refused to do so* — to their great credit, and to the credit of Pope Gregory VII who had trained[141] them so well.

---

139   Deirdre Manifold, *Fatima and the Great Conspiracy*, Militia of Our Immaculate Mother, 1992, pp. 39, 19-20.

140   February 12, 1112.

141   In this regard, historian Msgr. Philip Hughes says that, "The hard toil of the last sixty years, the labors and sacrifices of his predecessors, saved Paschal II." (*Op. cit.*, Vol. II, p. 313) And speaking in particular of Pope Gregory's excommunication of Henry IV, Hughes adds: "This act of unprecedented boldness, the culmination of the

The bishops recognized that following the Pope's order would be manifestly harmful to the Church, and they saw that their duty as bishops was to resist him. The bishops understood that the Pope's authority could not require such concessions from them, which would bring disaster to the Church, and they recognized that their duty was *not to obey* him in this. The reply of the Abbot of Monte Cassino says it all:

> "I love you as my lord and as my father, and I have no desire for another as pope. But the Lord has said, 'Whoever loves father and mother more than me is not worthy of me.' ... As for this outrageous treaty, wrung from you by violence and treachery, how can I praise it? Or indeed how can you? ... Your own laws have condemned and excommunicated the cleric who submits to investiture...."[142]

Another abbot wrote bluntly to Pascal that he deemed him a heretic. The Archbishop of Lyons rebuked the Pope, almost as strongly, "Detestable pilot that you are, in times of peace a bully and before the storm a coward." The Archbishop of Vienne (who was Pope Pascal's own legate in France), seconded by the Abbot of Cluny, wrote to the Pope:

> "If you hearken to our prayer and break with King Henry we shall be your faithful and devoted sons. If you remain in union with him, we pray God be merciful to us for we shall withdraw ourselves from your obedience."[143]

efforts of the reformers since 1049, was the culmination, too, of Gregory's reign, a focal point indeed of all the long history of the relation of the Catholic Church and the Catholic kings, towards which much previous history tended, to which all later history looks back. Gregory VII was to meet disaster upon disaster, to die with the Church divided, with the reformers defeated and scattered. But, because of the setting he gave it, this first papal excommunication and deposition of a king never left the Catholic memory. It fixed for all time, upon all subsequent popes and bishops, the elementary nature of their duty to secure the rights of religion — and in securing them to make no distinction of persons. '*Imperator intra ecclesiam non supra ecclesiam est*' [The emperor is within, not above, the Church]; so St. Ambrose had admonished Valentinian II seven hundred years earlier. St. Gregory VII's excommunication of the German king stamped that truth so deeply into Catholic practice that, henceforth, it ceased to be matter for discussion." (*Op. cit.*, Vol. II, pp. 303-304; Ch. 6, §1.) This principle of making no distinction of persons, of course, applies even to Popes, as the good bishops demonstrated.

142 Rev. Philip Hughes, *Op. cit.*, Vol. II, p. 313.

143 *Ibid.*, p. 314.

These good bishops' refusal to obey the Pope may seem scandalous to poorly informed Catholics today, who suppose that our duty as Catholics is to always obey the Pope unconditionally. We might do well to pause for a moment here to review what was said in Chapter 2 about our sometimes having a duty to resist authority.

Certainly the Pope has legitimate authority over us, and we have to obey him in all things *within his jurisdiction*. But (as these bishops understood) there are things that are not within the Pope's jurisdiction. No one, not even the Pope, has the authority to destroy the Church or to command us to do things contrary to the common good of the Church.

All authority in this world is limited. Only God has unlimited authority. St. Paul was called by Our Lord Himself to be an Apostle, and was given greater powers of personal jurisdiction than any bishop or Cardinal today possesses. But even Saint Paul recognized that his authority was limited. What is the purpose (and therefore the limit) of this authority that Christ has given to His ministers in the Church? St. Paul tells us that it exists for the building up of the faithful — for their edification — and *not for their destruction*:

> "[T]he Lord hath given us our power unto edification, and not for your destruction."[144]

The great 16th Century Dominican theologian Francisco de Vitoria discusses precisely this question of an unjust command of a Pope, threatening destruction to the Church:

> "[The Pope] does not have the power to destroy. Therefore, if there is evidence that he is doing so, it is licit to resist him. The result is that if the Pope destroys the Church by his orders and actions, he can be resisted and the execution of his mandates prevented."[145]

This is precisely what the German bishops did. They didn't go so far as to say, "We're going to start a new Church," or "We're going to depose the Pope." They just answered the Pope's order by saying, "No, we're not going to do that," and they carried on with

144   2 Corinthians 10:8.

145   *Obras de Francisco de Vitoria* (Madrid: BAC, 1960), p. 487.

their duties.

Paschal's mishaps did not end here, unfortunately — both for him and for the Church. Historians suppose naturally that Henry had foreseen the impossibility of the proposed settlement, and that he was taking advantage of Paschal's simplicity as well as of his weakness. When the temporalities could not be restored to him, Henry demanded in turn that Paschal formally and publicly restore to him the right of investiture, besides crowning him emperor.

Paschal rightly refused, and Henry abducted him (along with thirteen Cardinals) and returned to Germany. After two months of rough treatment in prison, Paschal again succumbed to Henry's demands and granted him the unconditional privilege of investiture.

Since the Pope's concession of the powers of investiture to the emperor had been made under duress, the Roman curia denounced the agreement as void. Scarcely a month had passed since his return to Rome before Paschal himself annulled the grant, declaring it to have been contrary to justice. At the same time (in the Lateran Synod of March 1112), he renewed the Church's previous decrees against lay investiture. The Council of Vienne, too, in October of the same year, declared Paschal's faint-hearted promise to Henry to be a *pravilegium* or "vicious law." It would have compromised the liberty of the Gospel established by Christ's command to teach all nations, free of encumbrance by temporal powers.

This incident of the German bishops' resistance to Paschal's unjust command is a perfect example of right-minded churchmen distinguishing between true and false obedience. They understood that when our reason and our Faith tell us that something is wrong, we can't be validly ordered to cooperate, even by the highest authority on earth. Yes, we must obey the Pope and our other ecclesiastical superiors *when they act within their jurisdiction*. Outside of that, we not only have *no obligation* to obey, but we have the *duty to resist* any falsehoods and injustices that they may try to impose.

To his own credit, Paschal publicly acknowledged his mistake, and not just at the Lateran Synod of 1112. Four years later, he publicly *cursed the day* that he had given his disastrous order to the bishops, and he congratulated them for recognizing that their duty lay in resisting him:

"I confess that I failed, and I ask you to pray God to pardon me. As for the cursed privilege, ... I condemn it with an everlasting anathema, and I will that its memory be forever hateful."[146]

A Pope Teaching an Error Against the Faith

Many Catholics misunderstand the Church's teaching on papal infallibility to mean that, *in all circumstances*, a Pope's teaching on matters of faith or morals is sure to be correct. That is not the case. We know, of course, that the Holy Ghost will never allow a Pope to *impose an error* upon the whole Church by a false *definition*, but at all other times a Pope *can be wrong* about the Catholic Faith, and he can even *publicly teach errors contrary to the Faith*, without any contradiction to the doctrine of papal infallibility. It can and has happened. Let's look briefly at one example of a Pope who "got it wrong," even about the Faith.

5) John XXII. Moving ahead again in history, this time by only 200 years, we come to the reign of Pope John XXII (1322-1334), who sparked a sizeable controversy over the Church's teaching about when departed souls enter into their reward or punishment in Heaven or hell.

Man is a composite creature, having both a body and a soul. We know that after a person's death, when his soul is separated from his body, the immortal and immaterial soul continues to exist and to act, even when the body has ceased to live. Nevertheless, the soul is not the essence of the whole man. Our natural state, as God created us, is to enjoy the living union of our body and soul:

"[The] soul without its body is incomplete; it is not fully itself unless it be united to the body. ... It is an extremely grave mistake to look upon the soul's presence in the body as a punishment, making the body a prison in which the soul serves its time. The body is good and a source of good to the soul joined to it; it is the one link by which the soul can attain its complete perfection."[147]

---

146 Lateran Council of March, 1116. Cited by Rev. Philip Hughes, *Op. cit.*, Vol. II, p. 314.

147 Rev. Walter Farrell, O.P., *A Companion to the Summa* (New York: Sheed & Ward,

The dead are therefore in an *unnatural* and *compromised* state while they await the General Resurrection.

This truth, taken to its extreme, might suggest to some that the souls of the departed (either for the sake of fittingness, or because of incapacity[148]) are forced to await the resurrection of their bodies before they receive their final reward or punishment in the next world.

This, in fact, was Pope John XXII's belief — that only after the Last Day would the souls of the just be given the intuitive "face-to-face" knowledge of God (the Beatific Vision). He also believed that the souls of the damned, and even the devils themselves, would not go into hell until after the General Judgment.

This was John's longstanding belief, and he had written a tract on this subject as Cardinal di Osa, before he was elected Pope in 1322. But it was not until fifteen years later, in 1331 (just three years before his death), that he made this topic a subject of his public teaching.

Pope John was preaching on All Saints Day, November 1st, in Avignon, France (where he resided instead of in Rome), and he spoke of the blessed as still awaiting their reward of Heaven, which would not come until they resumed the use of their bodies at the end of time. There was a considerable reaction, as you might suppose, and the Pope tried to substantiate and clarify his teaching in two other homilies, one given on December 15th, and the other on the following January 5th. But the more he tried to explain, the worse his situation became. The tradition of the Church was clear (though it had not yet been solemnly defined), that Pope John had gotten it wrong.

There rose up rightly a chorus of dissent, as theologians from well beyond the confines of Avignon rebuked the Pope for teaching heresy.

But the Pope also found some enthusiastic supporters of his errors. In any age, I suppose, there can be found "papaloters" who will follow the Pope into any novelty whatsoever. It happened in

---

1945), pp. 284-285.

148   Aristotle (*De Anima*, i, 4) seems to have considered disembodied souls as no longer capable of understanding anything at all, as Saint Thomas points out in his discussion of the knowledge of a separated soul (*Summa Theologica*, I, Q. 89, A. 1). Saint Thomas also shows how two statements of Saint Augustine might be misunderstood to mean that disembodied souls would not be affected by the corporeal fire of hell (*Summa Theologica*, Supplement, Q. 70, A. 3).

1331 that the recently elected head of the Franciscans, Gerard Ordon, was especially anxious to appear on the side of the Holy Father in any issue.

The former Minister General of the Franciscans, Michael de Cesena, had gone utterly head to head with Pope John over a question regarding the Franciscan Rule. The battle raged for more than a decade, until John finally not only excommunicated Michael, but even confined him to house arrest in Avignon until the end of his life. It is not altogether surprising, then, that the new Minister General of the Franciscans would make a fool of himself going to the other extreme:

> "The new head of the Friars Minor, the successor of the excommunicated Michael of Cesena, with sycophantic misunderstanding of the situation, became a most enthusiastic advocate of the pope's unusual views; and, unfortunately for himself, declaimed them at Paris, where he immediately fell foul of the greatest body of theologians in the Church."[149]

There was also another preacher in Paris at the same time, though a Dominican, who was championing the Pope's views. Together, these two mendicants started an uproar at the University of Paris. King Philip IV was in doubt about whether he should intervene, and the Pope wrote to him in November 1333 that since he (Pope John) had not meant to impose his teaching on the Church, there was to be no censure placed on discussions.

Theologians at the University of Paris convened for a formal consultation on the question in December 1333, and confirmed the teaching that the blessed are immediately admitted to the Beatific Vision after their death or their purification in Purgatory. They then asked the Pope to correct his error by confirming their findings.

Pope John responded at a consistory on January 3, 1334, with a public avowal that he had never intended to teach anything contrary to Sacred Scripture or to the Catholic rule of Faith, and that he did not intend to bind the Church to his belief. But he would not acknowledge the truth of those theologians' findings.

---

149 Rev. Philip Hughes, *Op. cit.*, Vol. III, *The Council of Lyons to Martin Luther*, pp. 191-192 (Chapter 2, Section 2, Part iv).

He then set up a panel of theologians at Avignon to consider the question in light of the writings of the Fathers. Chief among these theologians was the Cistercian Cardinal, James Fournier, who would very soon succeed John as Pope Benedict XII.

> "[Cardinal Fournier] was an extremely competent professional theologian, and without difficulty he clearly showed that the opinion of John XXII had scarcely any support and that the body of tradition was firm against him; on the other hand, in the controversy against those who, like Ockham, were beginning to denounce the pope as a heretic, Fournier noted first of all that, so far, the Church had never expressed its mind on the question by a definition, and next that in these three sermons John XXII had made no claim or pretense whatever to be doing anything more than preach a sermon to the particular congregation which at the moment filled the church; the pope had spoken simply as any bishop or priest might have spoken, as a private theologian, and not as the pope laying down a definition of doctrine for the assent of the whole Christian Church."[150]

It is unclear at this point whether Pope John remained unconvinced or if he was simply unable to give the matter further consideration. His final illness was upon him, and he would die on December 4th of that same year. But on the day before his death, he read aloud and signed before the Cardinals assembled at his bed, this (qualified) retraction of his former belief:

> "The souls of the just, separated from their bodies, but fully purified from their sins, are in Heaven, in paradise, with Jesus Christ, in the company of the angels. According to the common tradition, they see God and the divine essence face to face, clearly, as far as the state and condition of a soul separated from the body allow."[151]

It remained for the next Pope, Benedict XII, to finally settle the controversy started by John's erroneous teachings. On

---

150 *Ibid.*, p. 191.

151 Denifle et Clâtelain, *Chartularium Universitatis Parisiensis* (Paris: 1891), Vol. II, p. 441.

January 29, 1336, Benedict infallibly defined[152] the Church's true doctrine that the souls of the just are admitted to the intuitive, face-to-face Beatific Vision of God, either immediately after their death or upon the completion of their purification in Purgatory. In neither case must they await being reunited with their bodies at the General Judgment. Benedict's definition also established that the souls of the unrepentant sinners fall immediately into hell from the moment of death.

So we see in this final example of Pope John XXII, that a Pope can make mistakes not only in matters of prudence, but even in his beliefs and public teaching about the Catholic Faith. There is no guarantee of papal infallibility on all matters of faith and morals in a Pope's teachings *except when, following the conditions set forth by Vatican Council I, he is imposing a solemn definition upon the Church!*

Lessons for Our Times

So, yes, it is an historical fact that bishops and *even Popes and Councils can make errors* which are potentially disastrous for the Church, and which the faithful are bound to resist. Popes as well as bishops can and too often have failed in their sacred duty to defend the dogmas of the Faith, and a Pope can even *teach heresy in non-binding ways*. But the Church's dogmatic definitions can never fail. That is why God has provided us with these definitions through the infallible Magisterium of His Church, so that in times of crisis we will always be able to find the truth.

The Church's solemn and infallible definitions are absolutely accurate expressions of the Catholic Faith. They are our sure guide for knowing whether or not other doctrinal expressions are in agreement with — or contrary to — the Faith. Of course, we hope and expect to hear true Catholic doctrine from the theologians and bishops and Cardinals and Popes of the Church, but no academic degree or ecclesiastical rank is a guarantee of orthodoxy — not even in the case of a Pope. By a special grace, Popes are preserved from error *when they are defining dogma*, but at all other times even the Popes can fall into errors.

---

152 *Cf.* Pope Benedict XII, Bull *Benedictus Deus*, Dz. 530-531, D.S. 1000-1002.

There has been no lack of examples in our own time of false teachings being advanced by high-ranking Church authorities, and undermining the faith of vast numbers of Catholics. The faithful need to understand, for their own safety, that it is the *definitions* that carry the Church's timeless and authoritative guarantee of infallibility, not the latest utterances of those who happen to hold positions of authority in the Church. What the Holy Ghost has guaranteed through the Church's infallible definitions to be the true Christian teaching will always be true, regardless of whether or not future generations of Catholics — even churchmen — persevere in professing that true Faith. As St. Paul tells us,

> "What if some of them have not believed? Shall their unbelief make the faith of God without effect? God forbid."[153]

The failure of so many Catholics to grasp this distinction (between the Church's true authoritative teachings, as opposed to mere persons in positions of authority) is what has given such impetus to the confusion and divisions within the Church today. And this, in a few words, is what the Third Secret is about — the need to adhere to the defined dogmas of Catholic Faith, in spite of a growing apostasy having its roots in the bad example of many of the Church's upper hierarchy. Catholics must know and understand the dogmas of Faith (to the extent that we are able), and to live and defend them, in order not to be deceived by blind leaders in the Church who deny and undermine these dogmas.

---

153 Romans 3:3.

Avoid the Influence of Bad Pastors – Pray the Rosary, Cling to Dogma, Shun False Teachings

Remember to pray the Rosary, the Traditional Rosary, every day. Our Lady made 15 promises for the 15 Mysteries of Her Most Holy Rosary. In the 4th promise, She tells us that those who pray the Rosary every day will not fall into heresy. If they already had fallen there — if they continue to pray the Rosary — Our Lady will rescue them from heresy.

There is no doubt that the human element of the Church is afflicted today by "diabolical disorientation," to recall Sister Lucy's telling phrase. There is no doubt that the truths of the faith have been obscured in vast areas of the Church, leading to what even John Paul II called a "silent apostasy." In the Church today, Truth itself is in crisis.

In the first chapter of this book, I discussed our duty before God to love the Truth. In the second chapter I discussed how the Truth of our religion is found in the Church's infallible dogmatic definitions by Popes and Councils, and also in what the Church has taught for all time in Her universal and ordinary Magisterium, even without a formal, infallible definition (for example, the teaching on the evil of contraception).

The Church does not teach *novelties* of doctrine, for She has no power to invent new teachings. She has only the power *to preserve and defend the Revelation given to Her by Christ and the Apostles and handed down over the centuries in the Holy Bible and in the Sacred Tradition of the Church.* That is why the First Vatican Council, when defining the infallibility of the Pope in matters of Catholic dogma, warned that "the Holy Spirit was not promised to the Successors of Peter that by His revelation they might disclose new doctrine, but that by His help they might guard the revelation transmitted through the apostles and the deposit of faith, and might faithfully set it forth."[154]

Another way of putting this is that our faith is not based on what a priest, a bishop or even a Pope might say today, but only on what the Church has *always* taught and believed. Our faith is not announced in bulletins from the Vatican bureaucracy, but rather is contained for all time in what is called "the deposit of the Faith." It is that deposit — the Church's treasure of revealed truth — that is under ferocious attack today. And yet the promises of Christ are an absolute guarantee that the treasure of the Faith can never be stolen from us, changed into some counterfeit, or destroyed.

What this means is that we must *reject novelties of doctrine or dogma, no matter who presents them* and hold fast to what the Church has always taught, which can never change. But we must also hold fast to the Church's traditional practices, which support the truths of the Faith — above all the traditional liturgy of the Church. As Pope Saint Pius X declared in his great encyclical *Pascendi*:

> "But for Catholics nothing will remove the authority of the Second Council of Nicaea, where it condemns those 'who dare, after the impious fashion of heretics, to deride the ecclesiastical traditions, to invent *novelties* of some kind... or endeavor by malice or craft to overthrow any one of the legitimate traditions of the Catholic Church'....

> "Wherefore the Roman Pontiffs, Pius IV and Pius IX, ordered the insertion in the profession of faith of the following declaration: 'I most firmly admit and embrace the apostolic and ecclesiastical traditions and other observances and constitutions of the Church.'"

In the same encyclical Saint Pius X exclaimed: "Far, far from our priests be the love of novelty!"

Notice something about the quotation above: Saint Pius X affirms that the absolute commitment to "admit and embrace the apostolic *and* ecclesiastical traditions and other observances and constitutions" of the Church is part of the profession of Faith promulgated by Popes

---

154 Denzinger, 1836.

Pius IV and Pius IX, and affirmed by Saint Pius X himself. That is, the requirement of holding fast to *all* the traditions of the Church is itself part of the infallible Truth that cannot be changed or abandoned by any priest or bishop or even a Pope.

Notice also the reference to the Second Council of Nicaea. That Council *infallibly* defined the following proposition, and condemned for all time those who would reject it: "If anyone rejects *any written or unwritten tradition of the Church*, let him be anathema." Any means any. *Nothing* the Church has handed down can be rejected, despised, belittled or done away with by anyone in the Church, no matter how high his office.

So, we must hold fast to Tradition and reject novelty. But how do we know what is traditional and what is novel? Some people say that Catholics cannot judge this for themselves, that this would be "private judgment" like that of Protestants, and that we should just listen to whatever Church authorities tell us. That claim itself is false doctrine. Remember what Saint Paul told the Galatians: "But though we, or an angel from Heaven, preach a gospel to you besides that which we have preached to you, let him be anathema."[155] In other words, we must not listen *even to the Apostles or angels from Heaven* if they preach something other than the true Gospel.

And how do we know the true Gospel? The answer should be clear from the discussion in the previous chapters: We know the true Gospel from the infallible definitions by the Popes and the great Councils approved by Popes, and from what the Church has always taught even if there is no formal, infallible definition, for what the Church has always taught is infallible even without a formal definition. Our faith is a faith that the faithful can know themselves by reading what the Church has taught always and everywhere. We do not belong to some kind of cult whose teaching depends on the latest pronouncement of the cult leaders.

But where can we find these authentic, infallible teachings in a time of such great confusion in the Church? We can find them in the same sources that have always existed:

---

155   Galatians 1:6.

First, we can find the true doctrine of the Church in the teachings of the Popes and the Councils before the Second Vatican Council. Why not Vatican II itself? The answer is that Vatican II was the first and only Council that specifically *declined to teach infallibly*, and thus it did not teach infallibly (except where it repeated what the Church had always taught before). Recall the words of Cardinal Ratzinger, which I quoted in Chapter 2:

> "The Second Vatican Council… *defined no dogma at all*, and deliberately chose to remain on a modest level, *as a merely pastoral council…*"

We must, then, reject the claim that Vatican II "changed" any teaching of the Church whatsoever, for this is impossible. The Church cannot contradict Herself, because God does not contradict Himself. And if there were a contradiction between Vatican II, which did not teach infallibly, and the constant teaching of Councils and Popes before Vatican II, which *is* infallible, then Vatican II would simply be wrong. It is entirely possible for Vatican II to be wrong because it "defined no dogma at all, and deliberately chose to remain on a modest level, as a merely pastoral council…" In fact, this very decision to avoid clear, defined teaching in line with all prior teaching is where the "evil" of the Council lies, as I discussed in Chapter 2.

Second, we can find the true doctrine of the Church in Her great Catechisms approved by the sainted Popes, including the Catechism of the Council of Trent (approved by Pope Saint Pius V) and the Catechism of Saint Pius X, which contains all the essentials of our Catholic faith.

Third, we can find the true doctrine in the traditional forms of Catholic worship, prayer and devotion: the traditional Latin Mass, with its traditional Roman Missal, the traditional Breviary, the traditional Rosary, and in all the traditional prayers and devotions of the Church — including, of course, those devotions prescribed by Our Lady of Fatima: the Five First Saturdays and Communions of Reparation and the daily recitation of the Rosary. These forms of worship, prayer and devotion both contain and reinforce authentic Catholic doctrine.

Remember the fundamental principle: *lex orandi, lex credendi*. Loosely translated, this means that the way we worship determines what we believe. That is why belief is vanishing throughout the Catholic world today: traditional forms of worship have been abandoned. We must cling to these as tightly as we cling to true doctrine itself.

Yes, these are terrible times of disorientation in the Church. But, thanks be to God, our Church is not based on the merits or faithfulness of particular men, but on the Truth that makes us free and leads us to eternal salvation. Our Church is based on the Revelation of Jesus Christ, which has been preserved and handed down intact according to the promises of Christ, despite the failings of the Church's human element in various epochs, especially the one in which we live.

When the Pope and the bishops finally obey Our Lady of Fatima and consecrate Russia to the Immaculate Heart of Mary, the crisis in the Church will end and you will witness the Triumph of that Immaculate Heart over a rebellious world. Until then, until the wayward prelates of the Church return to the right path, you must "stand fast; and hold the traditions which you have learned."[156] For we have clearly entered into the time of Saint Paul's prophecy, "when they will not endure sound doctrine; but, according to their own desires, they will heap to themselves teachers, having itching ears: And will indeed turn away their hearing from the truth, but will be turned unto fables."[157]

Our Lady of Fatima, intercede for us!

---

156   2 Thessalonians 2:14.

157   2 Timothy 3:4.

Appendix

A Prophetic Interview with
Sister Lucy of Fatima

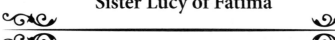

Introduction: This interview given by Sister Lucy to the Mexican priest, Father Fuentes, on December 26, 1957 is extremely important especially today. We see with the benefit of looking back over 55 years to the time of this interview just how accurate Sister Lucy was regarding the defections and betrayals of so many priests and nuns. This plea of Sister Lucy is today for us all even more timely than when she gave it in 1957. We should treasure and ponder this important message. It truly must be treasured because it is the last known public statement she gave before being silenced almost totally for the rest of her life. She died on February 13, 2005.

When it was first published by Father Fuentes it drew widespread interest from many of the faithful around the world. However, as a result of the courageous publication of this serious message, Father Fuentes received a totally unmerited and unprecedented persecution from some anonymous officials in the Diocese of Coimbra, where Sister Lucy lived.

In light of various similar events in the more recent past, in other Curias, we should not be too surprised to learn that a nameless official of the Curia in Coimbra on July 2, 1959 released a statement to the world press saying that the report of Father Fuentes was not true. Common sense, as well as the principles of law, inform us that a statement made by an anonymous official has no real authoritative value.

Father Fuentes Defended: In Mexico, the Archbishop of Veracruz, His Grace Manuel Pio Lopez, came to the defense of Father Fuentes. Cardinal Jose Garibi y Rivera, the Archbishop of Guadalajara, also publicly defended Father Fuentes against the unjustified attack of unnamed diocesan officials. Whoever these persons were who did this, we know that it could not be a Cardinal or Archbishop because there was no Cardinal or Archbishop in that Portuguese Curia. Neither did the authors of this grossly misleading statement of the Curia of Coimbra ever have the courage to identify themselves.

First Father Alonso, the official archivist for the Bishop of Fatima in 1971, adopted the "official" position of the Curia of Coimbra. However, he too, after studying the matter in depth came to the defense of Father Fuentes by 1976. He then said: "The authentic text, which in justice is the only one attributable to Father Fuentes, in my opinion contains nothing which gave rise to the condemnatory note of Coimbra. Much to the contrary, it reinforces a doctrine which is very apt to piously edify the Christian people."

Father Alonso had ample opportunity to speak to Sister Lucy from 1971 to 1976 so as to come to a more accurate understanding of this affair. He, by 1976, knew that neither Father Fuentes nor Sister Lucy has misled the world by this statement of 1957, which we have published below.

Sources: This matter has been documented at length by Frère Michel de la Sainte Trinité in Volume III of his series *The Whole Truth About Fatima*. The text published here is *The Fatima Crusader's* translation of the French and Spanish texts published in Frère Michel's book *The Third Secret* (Vol. III, pages 504-508).

The Report by Father Fuentes

"I wish only to tell you about the last conversation which I had with Sister Lucy on the 26th of December (last year). I met her in her convent. She was very sad, very pale and emaciated. She said to me:"

"No One Has Paid Any Attention"

"Father, the Most Holy Virgin is very sad because no one has paid any attention to Her message, neither the good nor the bad. The good continue on their way but without giving any importance to Her Message. The bad, not seeing the punishment of God actually falling upon them, continue their life of sin without even caring about the message. But believe me, Father, God will chastise the world and this will be in a terrible manner. The punishment from Heaven is imminent."

The Secret Not Revealed

"Father, how much time is there before 1960 arrives? It will be very sad for everyone, not one person will rejoice at all if beforehand the world does not pray and do penance. I am not able to give any other details because it is still a secret. According to the will of the Most Holy Virgin, only the Holy Father and the Bishop of Fatima are permitted to know the secret, but they have chosen to not know it so that they would not be influenced.

"This is the Third part of the Message of Our Lady which will remain secret until 1960."

Russia, the Scourge of God

"Tell them, Father, that many times the Most Holy Virgin told my cousins Francisco and Jacinta, as well as myself, that many nations will disappear from the face of the earth. She said that Russia will be the instrument of chastisement chosen by Heaven to punish the whole world if we do not beforehand obtain the conversion of that poor nation."

"The Decisive Battle" Between Mary and Satan:
The Falling Away of Consecrated Souls and Priests

Sister Lucy also told me: "Father, the devil is in the mood for engaging in a decisive battle against the Blessed Virgin. And the devil knows what it is that most offends God and which in a short space of time will gain for him the greatest number of souls. Thus the devil does everything to overcome souls consecrated to God because in this way, the devil will succeed in leaving the souls of the faithful abandoned by their leaders, thereby the more easily will he seize them.

"That which afflicts the Immaculate Heart of Mary and the Heart of Jesus is the fall of religious and priestly souls. The devil knows that religious and priests who fall away from their beautiful vocation drag numerous souls to hell... The devil wishes to take possession of consecrated souls. He tries to corrupt them in order to lull to sleep the souls of laypeople and thereby lead them to final impenitence. He employs all tricks, even going so far as to suggest the delay of entrance into religious life. Resulting from this is the sterility of the interior life, and among the laypeople, coldness (lack of enthusiasm) regarding the subject of renouncing pleasures and the total dedication of themselves to God."

That Which Sanctified Jacinta and Francisco

"Tell them also, Father, that my cousins Francisco and Jacinta sacrificed themselves because in all the apparitions of the Most Holy Virgin, they always saw Her very sad. She never smiled at us. This sadness, this anguish which we noted in Her penetrated our souls. This sadness is caused by the offenses against God and the punishments which menace sinners. And so, we children did not know what to think except to invent various means of praying and making sacrifices.

"The other thing which sanctified these children was to see the vision of Hell."

The Mission of Sister Lucy

"Father, that is why my mission is not to indicate to the world the material punishments which are certain to come if the world does not pray and do penance beforehand. No! My mission is to indicate to everyone the imminent danger we are in of losing our souls for all eternity if we remain obstinate in sin."

The Urgency of Conversion

Sister Lucy also said to me: "Father, we should not wait for an appeal to the world to come from Rome on the part of the Holy Father, to do penance. Nor should we wait for the call to penance to come from our bishops in our diocese, nor from the religious congregations. No! Our Lord has already very often used these means and the world has not paid attention. That is why now, it is necessary for each one of us to begin to reform himself spiritually. Each person must not only save his own soul but also all the souls that God has placed on our path.

"The devil does all in his power to distract us and to take away from us the love for prayer; we shall be saved together or we shall be damned together."

Last Times

"Father, the Most Holy Virgin did not tell me that we are in the last times of the world but She made me understand this for three reasons."

The Final Battle

"The first reason is because She told me that the devil is in the mood for engaging in a decisive battle against the Virgin. And a decisive battle is the final battle where one side will be victorious and the other side will suffer defeat. Also from now on we must choose sides. Either we are for God or we are for the devil. There is no other possibility."

The Last Remedies

"The second reason is because She said to my cousins as well as to myself that God is giving two last remedies to the world. These are the Holy Rosary and Devotion to the Immaculate Heart of Mary. These are the last two remedies which signify that there will be no others."

The Sin Against the Holy Spirit

"The third reason is because in the plans of Divine Providence, God always before He is about to chastise the world, exhausts all other remedies. Now, when He sees that the world pays no attention whatsoever then, as we say in our imperfect manner of speaking, He offers us with 'certain fear' the last means of salvation, His Most Holy Mother. It is with 'certain fear' because if you despise and repulse this ultimate means we will not have any more forgiveness from Heaven because we will have committed a sin which the Gospel calls the sin against the Holy Spirit. This sin consists of openly rejecting with full knowledge and consent, the salvation which He offers. Let us remember that Jesus Christ is a very good Son and that He does not permit that we offend and despise His Most Holy Mother. We have recorded through many centuries of Church history the obvious testimony which demonstrates by the terrible chastisements which have befallen those who have attacked the honor of His Most Holy Mother, how Our Lord Jesus Christ has always defended the Honor of His Mother."

Prayer and Sacrifice and the Holy Rosary

Sister Lucy told me: "The two means to save the world are prayer and sacrifice." Regarding the Holy Rosary, Sister Lucy said: "Look, Father, the Most Holy Virgin in these last times in which we live has given a new efficacy to the recitation of the Holy Rosary. She has given this efficacy to such an extent that there is no problem, no matter how difficult it is, whether temporal or above all, spiritual, in the personal life of each one of us, of our families, of the families of the world, or of the religious communities, or even of the life of peoples and nations, that cannot be solved by the Rosary. There is no problem I tell you, no matter how difficult it is, that we cannot resolve by the prayer of the Holy Rosary. With the Holy Rosary, we will save ourselves. We will sanctify ourselves. We will console Our Lord and obtain the salvation of many souls."

Devotion to the Immaculate Heart of Mary

"Finally, devotion to the Immaculate Heart of Mary, Our Most Holy Mother, consists in considering Her as the seat of mercy, of goodness and of pardon and as the certain door by which we are to enter Heaven."

Acknowledgments

First and above all, I offer my thanks to the Most Sacred Heart of Jesus, Who in His infinite love for me has continued to shower His graces upon me and my friends and associates and upon my efforts — despite my unworthiness, laziness and selfishness.

Next, to the Immaculate Heart of Mary, without Whose prayers and merits Jesus would have abandoned me long ago.

I thank all those who preceded me in promoting the Message of Fatima, and especially those who brought Our Lady of Fatima's story and Message to my attention and interest. Our Lady's prophetic Message will remain the defining and most crucial event of our lives, regardless of how much time remains to us — whether it be years or only a few months, days or hours.

I thank my parents, Malcolm and Jessie, my grandparents, and all the members of my family who gave me such good advice and example and helped me to foster a devotion to the Sacred Hearts of Jesus and Mary.

Thank you to all my friends, associates, co-workers, readers and supporters of the The Fatima Center Apostolate for their prayers, their donations and for their moral support of our limited efforts.

Thanks also to all those more than two hundred thousand souls who have touched my life, who have made The Fatima Center Apostolate and our Apostolic Outreach possible, and who have helped in any way to enable the grace of God and of the Sacred Heart of Jesus and the Immaculate Heart of Mary to achieve its purpose in making the Fatima Message known, understood, appreciated and obeyed, to the extent that has been accomplished thus far.

May all those mentioned above continue to help us from wherever they are to finally bring about the Triumph of the Immaculate Heart of Mary and the period of world peace that is certain to closely follow Her Triumph.

I would also like to acknowledge the invaluable assistance of the many editors, researchers, proofreaders and typesetters who have helped to shape this book in any way including: James Hanisch, Christopher Ferrara, Andrew Cesanek and the entire staff of The Fatima Center.

Thanks especially to the thousands of people who have assisted me by their prayers, and who continue to pray for me, and for this Fatima Center Apostolate.

Select Bibliography

Books on Fatima

Alban, Francis and Christopher A. Ferrara, *Fatima Priest*. Pound Ridge: Good Counsel Publications, Fifth Edition, 2013.

Fellows, Mark, *Fatima in Twilight*. Niagara Falls: Marmion Publications, 2003.

Ferrara, Christopher A., *False Friends of Fatima*. Pound Ridge: Good Counsel Publications, 2012.

----------, *The Secret Still Hidden*. Pound Ridge: Good Counsel Publications, 2008.

Kramer, Father Paul, *et al*, *The Devil's Final Battle*. Terryville: The Missionary Association, 2002, Second Edition, 2010.

Manifold, Deirdre, *Fatima and the Great Conspiracy*. Buffalo: The Militia of Our Immaculate Mother, 1992.

de Marchi, I.M.C., Father John, *The True Story of Fatima*. Fort Erie: The Fatima Center, 2010.

Martins, Father Antonio, *Documentos de Fatima*. Porto, 1976.

Michel de la Sainte Trinité (Frère), *The Whole Truth About Fatima*,

Volume I	*Science and the Facts*	(1989)
Volume II	*The Secret and the Church*	(1990)
Volume III	*The Third Secret*	(1990, 2001)

Buffalo: Immaculate Heart Publications.

Socci, Antonio, *The Fourth Secret of Fatima*. Fitzwilliam: Loreto Publications, 2009.

Walters, Bruce W., M.D., *Russian Sunrise*. Pound Ridge: Good Counsel Publications, 2011.

Books on Vatican II

Amerio, Romano, *Iota Unum: A Study of the Changes in the Catholic Church in the 20th Century*. Sarto House, 1996.

Brunero Gherardini, *The Ecumenical Vatican Council II: A Much Needed Discussion*. Frigento: Casa Mariana Editrice, 2012.

Graber, Bishop Rudolf, *Athanasius and the Church of Our Times*. Van Duren, 1974.

Kramer, Father Paul, *The Suicide of Altering the Faith in the Liturgy*. Terryville: The Missionary Association, 2006.

de Mattei, Roberto, *The Second Vatican Council: An Unwritten Story*. Fitzwilliam: Loreto Publications, 2012.

Wiltgen, Father Ralph, *The Rhine Flows into the Tiber*. Hawthorn Books, 1967.

Books on the Faith

Aquinas, St. Thomas, *Summa Theologica*. Allen: Christian Classics, 1981.

St. Charles Borromeo, *Catechism of the Council of Trent*. Imprimatur: Patrick J. Hayes, Archbishop of New York, 3 January 1923. Republished, Fort Collins: Roman Catholic Books.

The Catechism of Pope Saint Pius X. Gladysdale Victoria: Instauratio Press, 1993.

The Catholic Encyclopedia. New York: Robert Appleton Co., 1910.

Denzinger, Heinrich, *The Sources of Catholic Dogma*. London: B. Herder Book Co., 1957.

Denzinger, Heinrich and Schönmetzer, S.J., Adolf, *Enchiridion Symbolorum Definitionum et Declarationum*. Freiburg: Herder & Co., 34th edition, 1967.

...continued on inside back cover